Convicts, Codes, and Contraband:

The Prison Life of Men and Women

Convicts, Codes, and Contraband:

The Prison Life of Men and Women

Vergil L. Williams
Assistant Professor of Criminal Justice
The University of Alabama

Mary Fish
Professor of Economics
The University of Alabama

Ballinger Publishing Company ● Cambridge, Mass.
A Subsidiary of J.B. Lippincott Company

Library of Congress Catalog Card Number: 73-16233

International Standard Book Number: 0-88410-204-1

Printed in the United States of America

Library of Congress Cataloging in Publication Data

Williams, Vergil L
        Convicts, codes, and contraband.

        Bibliography: p.
        1. Prisons. 2. Prisoners. 3. Reformatories for women. I. Fish, Mary, joint author. II. Title.
HV8665.W48   365'.6   73-16233
ISBN 0-88410-204-1

To Lewis and Charles

*May his music play forever
and his horse never die*

Contents

List of Tables

Acknowledgements

As we have attempted to apply economic theory to the problems associated with the field of corrections, we have received two equally important types of assistance from our associates. Some years ago, Robert J. Brooks, Robert Dreher, Elmer H. Johnson, and Charles V. Matthews convinced us that the field of criminal justice was, by nature, an interdisciplinary undertaking and that we should bring our economic training to bear on correctional problems. In more recent years we have received the same type of encouragement from Frank R. Egan, Howard B. Gundy, and John C. Watkins, Jr. Without the vision and moral support of these men, we might never have ventured across disciplinary lines. They are, of course, to be held blameless for any errors we have made.

The second type of assistance that we have received is in the difficult arena of the day-to-day battle of manuscript preparation. We are grateful for the time and assistance made available by John S. Fielden and H. K. Wu in the College of Commerce and Business Administration, The University of Alabama. These two men also encouraged our interdisciplinary interests. And we certainly appreciate and here acknowledge the difficult typing, clerical and library research work done by Mary Ann Albright, Linda D. Barber, Sheldon Cox, Dora D. Howton, Linda Huff, Lee Lovey, and Anne N. Price.

Vergil L. Williams
Mary Fish

Foreword

Criminology draws on a wide range of social and behavioral sciences in attempting to explain those behaviors that subject individuals to the risk of imprisonment. It is remarkable that the criminological literature particularly fails to draw upon the intellectual resources of economics. In a thought provoking contribution toward filling this void, this book applies economic principles to the analysis of prison confinement. Among the justifications for giving serious consideration to this work, the book is a multidisciplinary examination of the inmate's sub rosa economy. Although they draw from the prison studies undertaken by representatives of other disciplines and utilize concepts such as role, status, organization, and community, Vergil Williams and Mary Fish are original in applying these studies and concepts to the analysis of an *economic* system.

An economic system, Williams and Fish explain, is composed of the organizations, network of institutions, practices, and beliefs of the given society that pertain to economic processes such as production, distribution, and consumption. These processes are universal in that—whatever the resources available, the state of the arts, and the level of technology—people convert their resources as efficiently as possible into those goods and services they need and want. This book applies the approach of economists to the study of the sub rosa economy that emerges from, and whose characteristics are shaped by, the placing of the prison inmate in the status of the economically underprivileged.

Several factors make the prison an island of poverty in which high demand is created for goods that would seem inconsequential or bizarre by free world standards: coffee, food, homosexual prostitution, alcohol, drugs, pornography, weapons, hot water, pressed trousers, and so on. Incarcerated offenders are systematically impoverished in economic, psychological, and social terms. Although provided basic subsistence without effort or uncertainty, they are denied access to those legitimate income-producing activities in prison which are the core of economic motivation in the free community.

Prison industries are hobbled by private entrepreneurs and labor organizations fearing competition from prison-made goods. Prison labor is justified more in terms of minimizing costs to the taxpayer and less in terms of inculcating work skills and aptitudes appropriate to meaningful employment of released prisoners. Because poverty is used as a fringe punishment appropriate to "enemies of society," the denial of goods and services expresses the outcast status of inmates, who thereby are encouraged to feel alienation from the standards supported by "rehabilitation" programs.

Truncated supply aggravates the demand for prohibited goods and services and motivates the rise of the sub rosa economy, which operates in secrecy to avoid detection, confiscation, and punishment by prison authorities in the course of those authorities' efforts to maintain internal order and to prevent escapes for sake of protecting the free community from "dangerous criminals." Although the authorities are prone to view inmate transactions as individualistic transgressions of official rules, Williams and Fish provide evidence of a complex and sophisticated economic system dedicated to meeting unfulfilled needs. This system comes in several versions.

The most elaborate version is the entrepreneurial clique under the leadership of an antisocial "right guy" who utilizes the techniques of ghetto hustling. Williams and Fish see the prison clique utilizing the methods, providing the services, and exhibiting the internal structure of crime syndicates. The right guy insulates himself from detection through lieutenants who are buffers between him and the workers. Aggressive inmates are hired as enforcers to maintain discipline. Other inmates are corrupters, obtaining the compliance of guards or inmates in strategic positions affecting access to needed goods and services. In and outside the prison, rackets involve gambling, narcotics, loan sharking, extortion, and alcohol.

In the self-producer/reciprocal trade variety, smaller scale activities are oriented toward raising living levels rather than straightforward entrepreneurship. The poor man in the free world grows food, manufactures objects, or performs services for himself as a means of countering the effects of marginal incomes. Similarly, some inmates achieve sufficient production to qualify as "merchants." Their economic activities are illicit according to official standards but lack the organizational skills and enforcement techniques of the clique leaders. Williams and Fish report that this merchant behaves much as the usual American entrepreneur operating in a situation of scarcity, but, of course, the official prohibitions and the peculiarities of the demand for goods and services affect the prison market structure. In pursuing profits, the prison merchant risks violation of the inmate code which prohibits exploitation of peers. In this respect, the merchant differs from the clique leader who has the advantage of being considered the "right guy" representative of the antiadministration values of the inmate code. Further, the clique leader is more sophisticated in concealing profit-making motives within the context of maintaining the inmate values.

Illicit economic activity in women's prisons, the authors say, occurs mainly within the context of "family" organizations, which include an approximation of all the roles of families in the free world. Because stealing rather than manufacture of illicit goods is emphasized, the females are typically more dependent than males on the staff's stocking goods that are available for theft. However, home-based skills are the basis of some manufacturing: sewing of clothing and "cooking" of alcoholic beverages, for example. In either stealing or limited production, the "family" is the economic unit in both the acquisition and consumption of illicit goods and services. Williams and Fish describe the family roles based on homosexual relationships; the "butch" adopts the male status in courting with gifts and, later, demanding tribute from "femmes" in an approximation of sex roles in the free world family.

This book is organized around several analytical themes that merit further exploration by several scientific disciplines. First, Williams and Fish repeatedly refer to the importance of the cultural backgrounds of inmates in shaping their choices among the three versions of economic activities described above. Socialization of personality and the division of labor are among the sociocultural patterns in free society that condition inmates to behave in certain ways in the pursuit of economic needs in prison. Ghetto hustling orients the right guy and his associates in choice of methods and services. The attitudes and adjustments of the self-producer stem from the experiences of the poor coping with problems of survival in the face of marginal income in the free society. Family roles and the status of females in American society generally are prototypes for sub rosa economic arrangements in women's prisons.

Second, the inmate businessman operates in an environment hostile to predictable outcomes of his transactions. Authorities endeavor to prevent and punish his illicit activities; they have the duty of denying him access to illicit goods and services, especially when theft of state property is involved. Inmate informers and business rivals create disasters for his planned operations. Payment of protection to dishonest employees and powerful inmates drain his profits. These handicaps and the very existence of an illicit economy in this hostile environment invite the economist's investigation of the conditions of the prison supply-demand equation that make possible the regularities of an illicit economy.

Third, in spite of the poverty of the inmate the sub rosa economic system, Williams and Fish conclude, is provided an adequate medium of exchange for maintaining a complex economic system. Although circulation of usual money is frequently prohibited and always sharply curtailed, inmates have access to funds from outside sources and canteen credit. Further, cigarettes are the basic illicit means of exchange. The availability of exchange demonstrates the impossibility of eliminating the sub rosa economic system and the viability of economic needs as a source of inmate motivation.

Fourth, regularized economic activities have important implications for assessment of the outcome of imprisonment as a societal response to the public problem of crime. The inmate social system, of which these economic activities are a crucial aspect; arises from the inmate resistance against the controls imposed by prison authorities. In generating inmate resistance, the prison establishment paradoxically opposes the rehabilitation goals it is supposed to achieve.

A key issue for students of prison organization is the identification of means of diverting inmate energy from resistance and into voluntary and self-fulfilling adherence to norms of legitimate society. The illicit economic activities constitute the mobilization of dedicated inmate energies which, if access to legitimate economic opportunity were provided inmates, could become the means of generating prosocial behavior. Especially in the case of the entrepreneurial clique, as Williams and Fish note, the sub rosa economic system reinforces the antiestablishment norms contrary to rehabilitation objectives.

The authors note that the source of the entrepreneurial clique's patterns and values may be traced to the structured denial of economic opportunity to ghetto groups in society in general. Thereby they suggest the wide range and profundity of research issues involved in the study of the economic implications of arbitrary punitive responses to the convicted offender. Certainly, crime prevention and reform of the prison should involve study of the possibility of developing structures of legitimate economic opportunities that would gain for rehabilitation programs the energies expended in the sub rosa economic system.

Fifth, in keeping with the above point, the authors cite the importance of "an inferior good." As an example, glue sniffing represents use of a product which is sought only because higher quality items are either not available or too expensive. Many of the goods and services of the sub rosa economy are demanded only because the prison has been deliberately made a place of poverty. The bizarre and antisocial nature of the illicit demand are produced by the very prison social system which is undermined by the sub rosa economic transactions.

The abnormality of prison life opposes the constructive return of the inmate to the free world. and this abnormality is derived from the social and economic poverty of the inmate. Provision of legitimate access to a "superior good" is a promising means of undermining the corruptive effects of the sub rosa economic system.

The reader is invited to discover additional implications of the findings of this book because the above comments are intended to provide only a sample. Perhaps the book's primary contribution is its documentation of the reality and vitality of this remarkable economic system. Other economists are invited to join this analytic effort.

Elmer H. Johnson
Professor of Sociology and Criminal Justice
Center for the Study of Crime,
Delinquency, and Corrections
Southern Illinois University at Carbondale

Preface

Notes on Methodology

Since the subject matter of this book involves research into the clandestine world of the prisoner, it seems appropriate to comment initially on the methodological problems encountered and the techniques employed to overcome these difficulties. Prisoners carrying on economic transactions within the prison sub rosa system—acts forbidden by the prison authorities—are punished, sometimes severely, if caught. Disciplinary action alone is enough to prohibit any discussion of the subject by incarcerated inmates, but even without this personal danger, inmates probably would not be willing to discuss their activities freely because of the inmate code or value system. An inmate, regardless of his personal attitude toward members of the prison administration, must live within the inmate social system and at least pretend to subscribe to the inmate code in order to insure his continued survival.

A chief tenent of the inmate code expressly forbids open coopera- tion with representatives of the free world. When one remembers that convicts are the rejected members of a society, it seems natural that they in turn reject the values of their keepers and seek acceptance within their own microcosmic society. These characteristics of the inmate population make the gathering of data on the sub rosa system rather difficult and make it necessary to resort to unusual methods in some instances.

The methodology employed in this study has four basic aspects. The first aspect, the most obvious and direct, is the traditional methodology used by sociologists who have written about the inmate society. It is simple observation of inmate populations over a period of time. The most sustained observation period occurred during the 1966-67 academic year when we participated in the educational program of Menard State Prison in Chester, Illinois. As extension teachers for Southern Illinois University, we commuted to the prison regularly and taught classes in political economy to inmates participating in the institution's educational program. During the time that we spent at this maximum security penitentiary, we had ample opportunity to observe the inmate subculture in operation, to associate with men serving time, and to discuss economic principles with these men. Since developing an interest in the economic facets of the inmate subculture we have watched for surface manifestations of the system during briefer visits to various state and federal prisons in the United States and in Europe. When one becomes aware of the nature and operation of the inmate social system, fragments can be observed even on short, casual visits to these institutions.

A second important technique employed draws upon the experience of penology practitioners and their observations of the inmate culture. During the 1967-68 academic year, the Center for the Study of Crime, Delinquency, and Corrections at Southern Illinois University received an Office of Law Enforcement Assistance grant from the United States Justice Department. The grant funded three eight-week training institutes for middle management correctional officers representing some sixty adult correctional institutions scattered throughout thirty states. These officers were developing curriculum and lesson plans that would be used to train new correctional officers entering their institutions. We were assigned the task of assisting these officers in developing plans for lessons dealing with the economic aspects of their institutions. As we began a literature search on the subject, we soon discovered a total lack of information dealing directly with the economy within the inmate culture. The literature on the formal economic system (those transactions sanctioned by the prison staff) seemed to be adequate, but little had been done with the informal, sub rosa system. We began the process of compiling our own information by making use of the substantial amount of direct knowledge and experience available within the group. The correctional officers' knowledge of the economic transactions occurring within the inmate social system was fragmentary, but the substantial range of agreement among them convinced us that the informal systems, like the social structures, do not vary greatly from one institution to another. Needless to say, discussions with these officers yielded important data constituting a valuable contribution to the present work. The information gleaned in this way has been helpful in understanding and in building a descriptive model of the system.

The third aspect of the methodology, although unusual, has proven to be as valuable as the first two techniques. The first two techniques provided the rough framework of the sub rosa system, but verification and systematic study that would confirm or deny the initial impressions was needed. By surveying a body of literature that is nontheoretical and non-academic, our goal was accomplished. More specifically, we read books written by inmates and ex-inmates. Free world citizens observing and commenting upon prison world denizens leave some credibility gap, however well qualified the observers may be. Given the inescapable fact that inmates are the only ones who know the extent and scope of economic activity within the inmate culture, the inmate perspective was sorely needed to check the accuracy of impressions gained by the methods already noted. One possible means of accomplishing this task, of course, would be for us to be incarcerated in a penitentiary to become part of this underground activity. But, as of this date, we have not been willing to probe into the subject that deeply.

Fortunately, another way to get the inmate perspective does exist and has proved to be fruitful. Some inmates and ex-inmates are not only capable and discerning, but also are prolific writers. They produce both fiction and nonfiction dealing with prison life in its many aspects. Their fiction is especially useful in adding richness of detail to the operation of the sub rosa system and particularly revealing as to the scope and extent of such activity. We recognize that fiction is not customarily used in a study of social science phenomena intended for presentation to the academic community. However, the study of operations conducted in secret calls for special measures and concessions.

As we plunged into the colorful but often grotesque world of this type of literature, we had the patronizing feeling that it was not a scholarly thing to do. Our attitude changed as we gradually came to grasp the significance of the inmate novels about prison life. The inmate who writes fictional accounts of prison life enjoys a special freedom of expression that is denied the inmate who writes nonfictional accounts. The fiction writer is freed of the inmate code that prevents him from being candid about activity in the prison. He merely changes names, dates, and places to protect the characters that he includes in his novels. If by chance he is pressed for information about the events depicted, he has only to say that the events are products of his fertile imagination. Thus he is free to describe the minute details of a prison murder, one he has witnessed as an actual event, without fear of any ill consequences to himself. He has complete freedom to describe the illegal economic activity of the prison. By selling it as fiction he does not betray the inmate code.

Inmates writing about life in prison and putting the experiences in the form of a novel can hardly neglect to draw upon true experiences of the inmate culture in which they have been immersed. In fact they are likely to represent situations in a fairly conservative way rather than exaggerating them because of the old adage: truth is stranger than fiction. The novelist endowed with professional skill is careful to give his work an air of credulity by maintaining a relatively conservative bent. After reading some of the more bizarre true accounts of prison life, events and actions minutely described by inmate writers have an unmistakable ring of truth. For example, recently a local newspaper pictured a primitive helicopter being painstakingly built piece by piece by inmates in an industrial prison shop. The pathos, the importance of the small, trivial events, the strength of the inmate code—indeed, the realities of the prisoner's life—perhaps can best be portrayed through the medium of the novel.

We are now convinced that inmate novels represent a better way to get the inmate's perspective of his society than does the standard interview. An interviewer is constantly in danger of being deceived by the shrewd inmate who has some personal goal or vendetta. Conversely, the goal of the inmate novelist is to tell a story about things he deals with and understands—the reality of prison life as the novelist sees and believes it. These novels are a ripe and fascinating source of material about the informal economic system, describing in many cases exactly how the forbidden activities are carried out despite the constant surveillance of the administration and the ever present threat of informers. The activities occur; this is not questioned. Almost any warden will show visiting dignitaries a collection of confiscated weapons illegally manufactured within the prison. In fact, the verification exists in the display. The inmate novel adds the richness of detail which provides us with the how and the why—for example, regarding the weapon manufacturing process—of many facets of their system.

The fourth feature of our methodology is a literature survey, including the more traditional reference to scholarly works. The excellent and growing body of literature on the nature of the inmate subculture is almost wholly the product of sociologists who have applied informal organization theory to the social context of the prison. Their works are generously sown with examples of social situations as they occur within the prison. We draw on their theories and examples. Although not studying the sub rosa economy systematically, they do refer to economic phenomena within the inmate culture. These references tend to be isolated remarks which are made as the author pursues some other train of thought.

The literature of economics contributes the basic principles which are a requisite to understanding the inmate social system. Certain economic principles operate in all systems, be it a rudimentary barter system of an isolated village on a South Pacific island, the sophisticated buying and selling actions of the New York Stock Exchange, or, in this case, the transactions carried on by inmates in prisons. Systems of production, consumption, and distribution, can nonetheless, best be understood when studied within their cultural context. Awareness of the mores, norms, and value systems of a particular society contributes to an understanding of the nature of the economy and the complex motivations inherent within it. Man does not engage in economic activity, an inevitable part of any society, solely to improve his material level of living. In addition to his material wants, man has a host of psychological and sociological wants—to love and be loved, to exalt himself, to attain recognition from his peer group and reference group, to display his uniqueness, and many others. Any or all of these behavioral variables may motivate him to engage in economic activity.

Very little of the economic literature deals directly with the economies that arise among the incarcerated. The one notable exception is a short article by R. A. Radford that appeared in the scholarly economic journal *Economica* in 1945. After being captured during World War II, Radford was placed in a prisoner of war camp. He described the economy that spontaneously developed in the camp. The article so captured the imagination of economists that it has become something of a minor classic in the economic literature and is still occasionally reprinted in reading books designed for beginning economics students. Despite their apparent fascination, economists have not pursued this line of inquiry.

Vergil Williams
Mary Fish

Chapter One

Cultures and Economies

When prison riots occur, public attention is focused on prisons for a brief interval of time. Articles, generally centering on the nature of the prison staff and physical facilities, loudly decry the inmates' plight. Exposés say guards are sadistic and ill-trained, food is poor, and recreational areas are inadequate. Still, few people, other than the incarcerated, are aware of the socioeconomic systems operative within the inmate society. Inmates in correctional institutions have a well-defined culture of their own that functions to provide prestige to the inmates—prestige that they are denied by the free world—and a sub rosa economy exists to feed and sustain it.

The inmate culture has its own values and codes. Inmate leaders emerge and disappear within the system, according to their ability to uphold its values and to usurp power from other inmates and officials. Prisoners outnumber the staff members of the institution that they inhabit, and inmate leaders, by virtue of the power accorded to them through the inmate culture, have considerable ability to control the inmate population. These leaders can use their influence to assure that the daily life in the prison proceeds peacefully or they, although seldom choosing to do so, can willfully, quickly throw the prison into an inferno of violence and turmoil.

This book is about the prison life of men and women: the way they organize their communities in order to provide for their physical, emotional, and social wants and needs—specifically, the way they operate illegal economic systems. The subject matter represents a very special microcosm. The social and economic relationships of prisoners is a type of microcosm because the society formed within the prison is, in a way, a small replica of the larger free world society in the United States. The sub rosa economy, a system within the microcosm, directly supports the social relationships and power structures of the prison society.

Prisons, reformatories, training schools, camps, halfway houses, diagnostic centers, jails, and workhouses comprise the United States correctional institution system. These places represent different vogues in naming places of confinement and diverse orientations according to the treatment philosophy or lack of it evident in any particular place of confinement. "Jail" is generally the name given institutions where the inmates serve one year or less, while other places mentioned, except halfway houses and diagnostic centers, generally house prisoners for periods longer than one year. This book is concerned primarily with the inmate culture as it exists within the institutions for persons serving one year or more. Appropriate United States directories list some 432 of these institutions with an average daily inmate population exceeding 400,000.[1]

It is necessary to elaborate on the scope of the material in this book because of the diversity of correctional institutions and their populations. Prisons, whatever they are named, vary primarily in the degree of security and control exercised over the prisoners—an important variation for the topic being considered, because the inmate culture is developed more definitively in institutions that exercise a high degree of control over the inmate. Tightly regimented institutions, by dehumanizing the inmate, cause him to be more dependent upon the inmate culture for his physical and emotional needs. Conversely, institutions that allow the inmate more freedom enable him to fulfill emotional and physical needs in ordinary contact with outside society. Inmate cultures and sub rosa economies are more evident in the prisons with a high degree of inmate subjugation.

MAXIMUM AND MEDIUM SECURITY PRISONS

The sub rosa economy described in this book is most clearly developed in maximum and intermediate security prisons for adult males and in prisons and houses of detention for adult females. Actually, the terms "maximum" and "intermediate" refer to both a type of construction and a degree of control. Male maximum security prisons are designed for prisoners who are considered to be unstable, dangerous, and in general rather high risk, either in terms of escape or aggressive behavior. Older maximum security prisons generally have imposing masonry walls surrounding the buildings on the grounds. Walls will be 18 to 25 feet high and have guard towers placed at strategic intervals along the walls. Newer maximum security prisons frequently have high wire fences that are more economical. Whether old or new, the maximum security prison is likely to make use of "inside" cells, a form of prison construction wherein cell blocks are constructed so that the cells are back to back with open corridors between the cell blocks and the outside wall of the cell house.

The maximum security institution, nevertheless, is best characterized in terms of regimentation rather than its architecture. Here inmates are subjected to continual surveillance by correctional officers who man the walls, officers who circulate throughout the population, and still other officers who monitor closed circuit television equipment. Inmates are counted several times each day; one count may scarcely be totaled before another begins. Inmates are frequently subjected to personal searches as they circulate within the institution. From time to time their cells are searched for contraband items such as guns, knives, and drugs. An inmate may be required to have a pass when moving from one section of the prison to another if he is not with a group of prisoners being accompanied by an officer.

The architecture of the male medium security prison is generally somewhat less austere. Cells may be built adjacent to a wall so that the cell window looks out into a yard. Regimentation and surveillance is slightly less rigorous. A number of prisoners may work outside of the prison under close supervision. Medium security institutions house inmates considered slightly more tractable and less dangerous than maximum security inmates.

The subject matter of this book is focused on male maximum and intermediate security prisons mainly because the relatively high degree of control and regimentation results in a well defined and developed inmate culture with a strong sub rosa economic system. Prisoners in minimum security prisons or in halfway houses, for example, have comparatively more freedom and tend to be less dependent upon the inmate culture to fulfill their needs. Thus it is in the male maximum and intermediate security institutions that one finds the well formulated sub rosa economic system.

Prisons for female inmates tend to be of the intermediate and minimum security types. Correctional administrators have never found it necessary to house female prisoners in highly regimented, maximum security prisons except in a few isolated instances where a branch of a predominantly male institution is used for females. Living quarters for female inmates tend to be cottage style (with individual rooms as opposed to cells) or dormitory type facilities. In general, women are subjected to a lesser degree of regimentation and surveillance because they have historically proved to be less prone to violence and escape, and too they are less feared by society.

Juvenile institutions are not considered in this study. In many cases, adult inmates have served time in juvenile institutions where they began learning the ground rules of the inmate culture. Although correctional literature confirms the existence of the inmate culture in juvenile institutions, these institutions are excluded here partially because we have had insufficient opportunity to study them and partially because of the discernible trend away from the practice of subjecting juveniles to the harsh penal provisions that produce a definitive sub rosa economy.

CULTURES AND SUBCULTURES

For the sake of brevity, the term "inmate culture" is frequently used; "culture" is a broad term that refers to the habits, customs, mores, values, beliefs, or superstitions of a body of people. As such, culture sets the general parameters for the social interaction which occurs among individuals. "Subculture" refers to a subgroup within a culture displaying some deviance from the generally accepted pattern of the culture. Since the inmates in our study are products of the culture prevalent in the United States, they are, strictly speaking, part of a subculture. For our purposes it is not important to distinguish between the terms "inmate subculture" and "inmate culture"; one finds both terms used in correctional literature. We use the terms interchangeably in referring to the values and beliefs of inmates or ex-inmates who have been subjected to incarceration as a result of a criminal offense.

The inmate culture exists as an entity in a dynamic social system. Criminals enter the inmate culture as a result of incarceration. Some inmates enter the system before they reach their majority and others enter during their wintry years. Eventually they leave the inmate culture one way or another: they are paroled, released after serving their full sentence, or they die in the institution. Wardens, correctional officers, and rehabilitation personnel all eventually retire, are fired, or quit to move on to greener pastures. In short, individuals enter the system, become an active part of the system for varying intervals of time, and ultimately leave the system. Quickly recognizing upon their entry into the institution that the inmate culture exists and that it will still exist when they leave the institution, participants accept its stability. Furthermore, the inmate culture exists in the same basic form in prisons that are widely separated by distance. California's inmate organizations are not much different from those of Maine, Iowa, or Alabama prisons.

CONCEPT OF A PRISON COMMUNITY

A community consists of individuals who are unified for a host of reasons, for example, because of living in the same area, of sharing common interests, or of coming from similar backgrounds. Obviously, communities are established on a number of bases; for instance, membership in the American Kennel Club or the Holt High Parent Teachers Association involves sharing specific activities and, therefore, constitutes one possible base for a community. A community may be forged by a sharing of territorial privileges such as residence in Southwood Lake or Heritage Hills housing development makes one a community member.[2] Prison inmates share both territory and activities, thus they form a community, although to say the least, their territory is generally limited to a few acres and they have a limited choice of activities. Such limitations cause them to come into contact with one another more frequently than would the residents of Southwood Lake and to participate in the same activities more frequently than would the members of the Holt High Parent Teachers Association.

— The inmates' close proximity to one another helps to perpetuate the inmate culture. Culture is transmitted from one inmate to another; as they engage in verbal and nonverbal communication within their community, its basic tenents are consciously or unconsciously assimilated. Inmates incarcerated within a particular institution share the common goal of survival. Survival requires a degree of cooperation and conformity. As a member of a prison community, the inmate learns about the inmate culture and gradually becomes a part of the culture; then he helps to transmit it to others.

ROLES, STATUS, AND USE OF ARGOT

An individual inevitably has some status in every social group of which he is a member. In a group the status of every member is determined by his relationship with every other member of the group. In turn, groups have status in relationship to other groups. It is the myriad associations with others that make the individual what he is, or more precisely, what he thinks he is, for an individual's concept of himself is largely based upon his status in his social groups.

Formal, recognized organizations all give names, titles, or labels to people who are cast in certain roles, who perform designated functions, or who have special authority and power. One finds this demonstrated in a variety of organizations; a few examples: military units have generals, Southern Baptist Churches have deacons, universities have professors; and the Eastern Star has worthy matrons. This titling and labeling process is duplicated in informal organizations just as it operates in formal structures. The inmate culture assigns names and roles to its members as well.

Both a formal and an informal organization are always present in a prison. The formal is properly authorized, recognized, and sanctioned by the state. Distinguishing roles are assigned staff members of the institution responsible for the custody, care, and rehabilitation of the prisoners. Labels that give some indication of the status of the position accompany all roles. For example, the term "warden" immediately conveys to all concerned parties that this person occupies a high status position, one who wields power. Conversely, the term "guard" connotes a low status position, with little power and no prestige. Treatment professionals employed by the institution have titles derived from their particular qualifications—titles that also convey degrees of status. The term "psychiatrist" denotes a high status position; while the term "social worker" implies a relatively lower status position because that title can be earned more easily than the psychiatrist title. Inmates, being the product of the formal system, are accorded no status other than as "objects."

In juxtaposition to the formal, a prison also has an informal organization; more precisely, several informal organizations may exist among both the staff members and among the inmates. Here, however, our concern is centered on the informal organization of the inmates. As already mentioned, the titling and labeling process occurs in this informal culture as with the more formal. Inmates also have names for individuals who perform unique functions or who have power and authority. Taking the form of prison argot (slang terms), labels help to define the relationship among inmates.

This principle can be illustrated by using an analogy from the free world. Jemison, a businessman, introduces himself to Hultry, another businessman, on a domestic flight from New York to Chicago. Both men feel vaguely uncomfortable after exchanging names. After a few moments, Jemison tells his new acquaintance that he is a producer of plumbing fixtures from Milwaukee. Hultry volunteers that he is a distributor of electrical light fixtures operating out of Aurora. Then, both men feel more relaxed because they have defined their roles and know how to react to one another. In a slightly different manner, a similar defining of roles occurs in prison. Shorty introduces Billy, a new prisoner, to Fatso. After moving beyond Fatso's earshot, Shorty tells Billy that Fatso is a "real man"—indicating that Fatso occupies the high status position of a leader in the informal inmate organization. If necessary, Shorty explains in detail the significance of being a real man. Thereafter, Billy knows how to react to Fatso. Meanwhile, Fatso has perceived that Billy occupies the status of a "fish"—indicating that Billy's qualities are still unknown and that he must be subjected to a period of testing before his role and status are clarified.

The social roles, designated and labeled by the inmates, form the basic structure of the social relationships built by the inmates as a response to the problems of confinement.[3] An inmate who is assigned a role tends to act out that role. This tendency is no different from the behavior of a person outside of the prison. For example, a man may temporarily assume the role of a scoutmaster for a Boy Scout pack, neckerchief and all. The scoutmaster has a reasonably clear-cut idea of the traits that a scoutmaster should exhibit: he should be patriotic, he should be truthful, he should be an outdoorsman, and so on. Once the scoutmaster has mentally reviewed the characteristics of his status position, he has defined his role and begins to exhibit these expected traits when in the presence of his scout pack. Inmates act out roles in much the same way; however, one inmate may play one role at one period of his incarceration and play an entirely different role at a later time during the same incarceration interval.[4]

AN ECONOMIC SYSTEM

Economics is concerned with the nature and operation of economies. If one uses a conservative definition, economics is the study of the way people allocate available resources among alternative uses. More specifically, as a topic of investigation, it deals with resources, man, technology, and the "economizing process." Simply, the economizing process is universal in that whatever the resources available, state of the arts, and level of technology, people convert their resources as efficiently as possible into those goods and services they need and want. Actually, society's resources, technology, and cultural values form the constraints within which alternative economic choices are formulated or, to say the same thing in another way, determine the available alternatives.

An economic system is used to provide for the material goods and services that satisfy social, psychological, and physiological wants. But more than this, an economic system is the organizations, network of institutions, practices, and beliefs of the society that pertain to economic processes such as production, distribution, and consumption. An economic system subsumes those functions and orderly procedures that people invent and use with the economizing process. The system sets forth the ways in which people will interact when carrying on economic activities.

The sectors of a simple economic system, business and household, consist of individuals and/or groups who at one time play the role of producer and another, consumer. A production unit is an individual or group, commonly called a firm, which produces goods and services, while a consumption unit is an individual or a household (a family, for instance) that consumes goods and services.[5] Individuals in a breadwinner role tend to be a part of both a production unit and a consumption unit because they acquire income for spending on consumption by participating in the production process. But an economic system is not necessarily a one-tract, two-sector system; several spheres of economic activity may exist, and each sphere may operate differently while still remaining part of the whole. For example, in the United States we have a profit sector and we also have a nonprofit sector comprised of units such as several levels of government and private foundations.

The activities of an economic system can be divided into three basic processes: production, consumption, and transfer. The production process includes the making of goods and the rendering of services. Both consumer and capital goods are produced. Whereas consumer goods—for example, a hamburger, an automobile, or a television set—provide the purchaser with direct satisfaction, capital goods, such as machines, buildings, and trucks, are used to produce consumer goods. The capital goods are used to enhance the efficiency of producing consumer goods that do give direct satisfaction. Consumption is the process wherein goods and/or services are consumed or utilized either directly for personal satisfaction or indirectly through the using up or wearing out of goods. The transfer process includes actions such as sales, purchases, exchanges, barters, borrowings, lendings, and even theft and appropriation. Transfer events are the links between and among the production units and the consumption units in the structure of an economic system.[6]

The specific structural characteristics of an economic system and the specific nature of the processes that take place will depend upon the physical and social environment—raw materials, technology, and culture. Economic activity is not set apart nor does it occur in a vacuum; rather it is inextricably interwoven with the other aspects of society. Although often remarkably similar, economic organizations are established to deal with unique environmental conditions. Because economic organizations are always developed within a social framework, they channel economic choice according to established goals and norms of society; moreover society, by confirming individual choices, gives them a basic meaning.

Be aware that the social framework of an economy does far more than set forth laws and regulations; it provides meaning and values for an economic system. Prison inmates have needs that are often cultural rather than nutritional, a topic discussed in later chapters. Social conventions, religious beliefs, and ethical and moral codes shape the wants and desires of any society. Even economies operating at a subsistence level demonstrate the importance of culture; but for those above this level, cultivated factors become more important. Above abject poverty, the individual's economic behavior focuses upon actions that will strengthen his social standing and enhance the attainment of his social aspirations.[7]

FORMAL AND INFORMAL ECONOMIC SYSTEMS IN PRISONS

Every prison has an economic system which is recognized, sanctioned, and in fact established by the prison authorities. Components of this formal system include the prison factory, the prison farm, and the prison commissary. The formal system provides a means for inmates to obtain income legally by working in the prison industry, by doing handicrafts, by receiving gifts from outside the prison, by depositing accumulated wealth at the time of commitment, or by working outside the prison in a work-release program. This sanctioned system also provides means by which the inmate can legally dispose of his income: spending it on a limited range of consumer goods at the prison commissary or sending money to his relatives in the free world.

The formal economic system of a prison operates as a part of the rigorous controls exercised over the inmate's life. The legal income that he can earn inside the prison is severely limited by the low wages paid in prison industry. The amounts that he can spend at the prison commissary are carefully controlled by establishing a monthly or weekly maximum limit. Even amounts that he can spend from earnings in a work-release program are subject to limitations; he must save a part for his release, send a portion to his family if he has one, and pay the institution a portion of his income for his room and board. We call this highly structured and authority-sanc-

tioned economic system the formal economic system of the prison in order
to distinguish it from the informal economic system or sub rosa system
that is the primary concern of this book.

The formal economic system of the prison is carefully planned and
strictly controlled by prison administrators partially because of security
considerations and partially because of society's general attitude concerning
inmate life styles. The security of the prison unquestionably requires strict
control of the form of inmate wealth. Contraband such as civilian clothes,
weapons, and free world money enhance the possibility of a successful escape.
More significantly, the formal economy also is curtailed because poverty is
considered to be an appropriate condition for the incarcerated. Poverty is a
fringe punishment. Our society also exhibits a considerable amount of ground-
less fear that the inmate may come to feel that he is "better off" in prison
than he was "on the streets" if he is allowed to develop his maximum
economic potential.

These attitudes are reflected in the strict control of inmate
expenditures exercised at the prison commissary. Commissary visits are
allowed at regular but relatively infrequent times, and an inmate can spend
only a limited amount at the commissary during these specified time intervals.
For example, some state prisons in Alabama allow an inmate to spend $12.50
per week at the commissary—a fairly typical sum. This sum is not large
considering the multitude of amenities of life which the prison does not
provide the inmate. And the range of consumer goods available at the commissary is severely limited. A typical commissary stocks a few food items,
tobacco, toilet articles, some articles of underwear, towels, bedding and
perhaps some hobby equipment. Correctional personnel, reflecting the general
attitudes of American society, believe that inmates are not entitled to an
abundance of consumer goods. . ."After all, a prison is not the Regency Hyatt
House in Atlanta!" In addition, purchase of consumer goods at the commissary is viewed as a privilege which may be withdrawn if disciplinary measures
are to be invoked.

In maximum security and medium security prisons, where
surveillance of the inmates is continuous and restrictive, security precau-
tions prohibit the circulation of United States government currency (and coins
in some instances). Currency represents a security threat because it can be
used to corrupt guards and to purchase materials needed for a successful
escape, or because internal strife, often of severe dimensions, may be created
by thefts and extortion. Inmates in these institutions generally have their
money handled as "book credits" against which they may draw for the
limited expenditures they are allowed to make.

The formal economic system is not the main topic of this book,
however; the underworld economy is. Practically all corrections literature that
mentions a prison economic system deals directly with the formal economic

system, while the informal or sub rosa system has escaped the attention of most researchers and writers. The secrecy and complexity of the informal economic system make it a topic that is little understood. Most researchers in correctional institutions, being trained in sociology or psychology, have been concerned with other aspects of the inmate culture. And few economists have delved into the nature of economic behavior among institutionalized offenders.

The "informal" or "sub rosa" economic system are terms used in this book to indicate that the topic of primary interest is the illicit economic activities that occur in the inmate culture. This distinction is necessary in order to separate our subject matter from the regular and ordinary discussions of fiscal matters of concern to prison administrators who are responsible for the operation of the formal economic system of the prison. The transactions of the sub rosa economy are generally prohibited by the prison administration, although they may be quietly tolerated. Since these transactions are of the nature of forbidden fruit, they must be negotiated and conducted in secrecy to avoid detection, confiscation, and punishment by prison authorities. Officials frequently do see evidences of such secret transactions and do from time to time interrupt the activities, but those involved are prone to view such acts as individual violations of prisons rules, not as part of a complex and sophisticated economic system which serves the needs of a group of offenders who, sequestered from free society, have built a society of their own within the geographically compact area of a prison.

RATIONALE FOR STUDY

Aid to Correctional Practitioners

The penitentiary serves two broad functions: custody and rehabilitation. For correctional practitioners, a knowledge of the informal economic system is helpful in attempting to fulfill both functions; but for the sake of clarity we will consider each function in turn.

The custody function of the penitentiary requires that convicted offenders be protected from each other and be isolated and separated from the larger society by maintaing them in a restricted geographic area; society is protected from dangerous offenders and offenders are kept in a centralized location where they can be subjected to treatment and rehabilitation procedures. To accomplish this function, correctional personnel are expected to prevent escapes of those inmates inside the walls and to minimize the number of "walk-aways" of inmate trustees who work outside of the prison or who are committed to minimum security prisons. Offenders sentenced to institutions, in short, must be forcibly detained until they are pronounced rehabilitated or their sentence is completed. But the custody function also involves the obligation to maintain an orderly and safe society within the prison. Once the state deprives a person of his freedom, it incurs legal responsibilities to provide for his health and personal safety because he is legally presumed to be incapable of making his own provison for these essentials. Thus custody also involves protecting the inmate from other inmates.

Escape attempts are not as common as the general public would believe. Attempts to escape do involve considerable personal danger to the inmate since most state statutes not only authorize the legal killing of convicted felons attempting to escape, but also require custodial personnel to follow this guideline for the protection of the general public. In addition to the danger of getting shot, there is the threat of an additional sentence being imposed if the inmate is caught and returned to custody. These practices act as a deterrent for most inmates since the majority have a reasonable expectation of being released within a few years. Escape attempts do occur, nonetheless, and it is reasonable to suppose that many escapees are desperate or unstable individuals who feel that they have little to lose. Under these circumstances they pose a significant danger to society and an important threat to fulfilling the custody function within the prison.

Successful escapes require contraband items not available to inmates through the channels of the formal economic system in the prison. One critical item is civilian clothing. Prison issued clothing is distinctive enough to make hiding difficult, particularly in the immediate vicinity of the prison where the populace is constantly on the alert for possible escapees. Acquisition of a piece of civilian clothing enhances an inmate's chances of making a successful escape. Other contraband items such as currency and road maps, may improve his escape potential as well. Contraband items can be acquired in the sub rosa economic system, especially if the correctional officer is not alerted to both the possibility and the operational techniques inmates use. The following chapters will demonstrate the inmate's ability to obtain such contraband by participation in the informal economic system.

An inmate, if he is so inclined and has some talent, can become wealthy and powerful by convict standards; and he can use his wealth and authority to manipulate, abuse, and exploit fellow prisoners. Custodial officials should be able to control this type of exploitation and the potential violence that it portends, but control requires a knowledge of the manifestations of this exploitation and the techniques by which it is accomplished via the sub rosa economic system.

Aid to Treatment
The therapeutic idealogy has gained acceptance in the correctional field, maintaining that the offender is "sick" due either to psychological or social pressures: because of his "illness" the offender became deviant, which ultimately led to his incarceration.[8] It logically follows that the proper function of prison personnel (in addition to their custody function) is to

diagnose and treat the offender's "sickness." Thus the rehabilitation function of the prison carries the responsibility of treating the inmate and restoring him to society as a well person who will no longer be deviant. This process has been designated by a number of terms: reformation, rehabilitation, or resocialization are a few commonly used. Whatever the particular term in vogue, the treatment is focused on the personal qualities of the individual.

The therapeutic ideology has triggered a vast amount of research which is concerned with the behavior patterns of offenders in order to gain the type of understanding of criminal behavior that will allow the formulation of an effective treatment strategy. Plans obviously cannot be fully and effectively developed without at least a limited understanding of the motivation forces behind human behavior. A part of this type of research deals directly with the inmate culture: the social system of institutionalized offenders is studied to isolate the values, behavior patterns, or mores that develop as a response to incarceration. One might tend to suspect that a group of rebels—muggers, rapists, forgers—confined together would exist in a perpetual state of anarchy. Far from the case; The inmate society is surprisingly orderly and organized.

Since the therapeutic philosophy calls for a study of behavior patterns of man in a particular social situation, the economic aspects of such behavior should not be neglected for they represent a significant part of his daily behavior. Economics is a behavioral science that attempts to describe human behavior in man's ordinary day-to-day activity as he copes with the dozens of wants that arise due to his physical and psychological needs. The sociologist concentrates mainly upon man's behavior as he reacts to other men, his behavior as a response to the presence of others who form some type of group or unit. The economist concentrates upon man's reaction to an environment of limited resources. Using the terminology of economics, the economist studies the ways in which man cooperates with other men to fulfill as many of his wants and needs as possible. In some ways the two disciplines are closely related, and at times interwoven so as to be almost indistinguishable. Still, the sociologist and the economist have different orientations, which result in one seeing relationships that the other might not see immediately. For this very reason, cross-disciplinary approaches to problem solving are frequently useful.

Aid to Economists

The particular problem at hand—the study of the behavior patterns of institutionalized offenders—can be strengthened and enriched by the addition of information concerning the economic behavior of inmates. Such additional information is an adjunct to the work already completed on the inmate culture. While treatment strategy is enhanced by any addition to the cumulative body of knowledge on human behavior, an understanding of the sub rosa economic system of prisons will help to formulate particular types of treatment strategy that will aid the correctional practitioner in performing the rehabilitation function, in addition to contributing to the general understanding of social behavior.

The contemporary student of economics is faced with the intricate task of attempting to understand the vast and complex economic systems of the nations of the modern world. As the body of economic knowledge has increased, a high degree of specialization has become necessary, as with other disciplines. Specialization allows the study of economics to proceed in an orderly fashion, but it has an unfortunate side effect for the beginner. He must attempt to correlate the principles and specialized training (perhaps in microeconomics and macroeconomics) as well as to apply them to the real world. He desperately needs an example compact enough to be visualized in order to see the application of the basic laws and principles of the operation of economies.

The prison can provide this example for the student of economics. Although not identical, the prison is a relatively compact society in miniature. As a society in microcosm the prison has an economy in microcosm that is small enough in scale for the economics student to grasp, provided the shroud of secrecy can be lifted sufficiently to allow its operation to be visible. This book attempts to lift that cloak of secrecy sufficiently to make the work useful to the student struggling to understand the basics of economic systems.

More advanced students of economics are interested in the philosophical issues of comparative systems. Given that an economic system arises in a prison, what form will it take? Will the inmates simply copy the capitalistically oriented system owing to the fact they are most familiar with that type of economic organization? Or, since it seems unlikely that individual inmates are aware that they are building an economic system, will the sub rosa economy take on the characteristics of a primitive barter economy? On the other hand, prisons now contain many "political prisoners" who have been incarcerated because they are dedicated to a form of political-economic philosophy calling for the violent overthrow of capitalism. Being relatively well read, well educated, and verbal, these prisoners are able to teach their doctrines to inmates belonging to extremely alienated ethnic groups who are searching for an alternative way of life. One finds a considerable amount of Communist dogma being expounded in America's contemporary prisons. Does this imply that the sub rosa economic system might take on the characteristics of a socialist economy?

Nations of the world elevate their economic philosophy to a way of life. That is, a country indicates that its economic affairs shall be arranged primarily in a capitalist or socialist form of organization, and this decision is taken to imply the acceptance of a broad range of political ideologies, deeply affecting the life style of the citizens of that country and having international implications in the lineup of Communist block and Capitalist block nations.

It is unlikely that the inmate has a desire to elevate his sub rosa economic system to the status of a political ideology; it is even unlikely that he perceives that he has an economy. He is certainly aware of illicit economic transactions within the inmate culture, and he is likely to participate as a consumer or producer many times during his incarceration. Even so, the inmate's awareness of economic transactions and his participation do not by any means indicate that he is aware that these events have interrelationships characteristic of a complex economic system. This latter position is equivalent to the argument that the economic system in the inmate culture arises without any deliberate application of theoretical principles; whereas it clearly arises spontaneously, in response to a need. Such a spontaneous economy—if indeed it is that—is divorced from political ideologies and is completely "natural."

The student of the comparative economic systems will be interested in discovering the answers to the questions posed in the above paragraph. Institutional economists will be interested in the shape an underworld economy takes in response to the cultural background of the prisoners—the impact of culture on the particular form an economy will assume. The following chapters will illustrate, for example, that the sub rosa economic activity in women's prisons is substantially different from illegal economic activity in prisons for males. Perhaps the type of economic system adopted by a society depends greatly upon the cultural backgrounds of the members of that society.

Economists should not be too eager to regard the sub rosa prison economies as vignettes of the United States economy. True, numerous criminologists, sociologists, and penologists point out that a prison is a society in microcosm, and that as such it is a social laboratory. It is also true that a prison community is a small scale society bearing some characteristics of the free society in which it is located. But there are important differences. Islands of private enterprise operate surreptitiously in a police state. Henry Burns, Jr. points out that a prison society has all of the characteristics of a totalitarian state.[9] Keeping this in mind, insight into the inmate sub rosa economy may give economists and political scientists clues as to the operation of a controlled society, as well as insight into a free society.

SUMMARY

The purpose of this chapter was to define the nature of the subject matter and to give brief sketches of key concepts necessary for the understanding of that subject matter. In addition, we have delineated the possible usefulness of the material for the field of corrections and the place of the findings in the academic study of economics and political systems. Before proceeding to the economic dimensions of the inmate culture, the reader could profit by a synopsis of the basic nature of the inmate culture—what it is and how it has been studied. Chapter 2 is a brief survey of that particular body of literature which has grown up around the concept of an inmate culture. Academicians who are already intimately familiar with that body of literature may wish to proceed directly to the material in Chapter 3 that describes the underworld economy of male prisons.

Notes for Chapter 1

1. U. S. Department of Health, Education, and Welfare, *Correctional Institutions,* vol. 2, by Herman Piven and Abraham Alcabes, no. 565 (Washington, D.C.: U. S. Government Printing Office, 1969), pp. 4-5.

2. Donald Clemmer, *The Prison Community,* rev. ed. (New York: Holt, Rinehart and Winston, 1958), pp. 87-88.

3. Rose Giallombardo, "Social Roles in a Prison for Women," *Social Problems* 13 (Winter 1966): 285.

4. *Ibid.*

5. Edward E. LeClair, Jr., "Economic Theory and Economic Anthropology," in *Economic Anthropology: Readings in Theory and Analysis,* ed. Edward E. LeClair, Jr. and Harold K. Schneider (New York: Holt, Rinehart and Winston, 1968), p. 200.

6. *Ibid,* pp. 201-202.

7. *Ibid,* p. 43.

8. Elmer H. Johnson, *Crime, Correction, and Society* (Homewood, Ill: Dorsey, 1964), pp. 320-321.

9. Henry Burns, Jr., "A Miniature Totalitarian State Maximum Security Prison," *The Canadian Journal of Corrections* 9 (July 1969): 153-164.

Chapter Two

The Inmate Culture

Prison culture has been a distinct topic of study since the Great Depression of the 1930s when an extraordinary sociologist, employed by a state prison, began to analyze the social relationships of inmates in terms of social stratification and informal organization theories. Donald Clemmer's pioneering work served to introduce his colleagues to the existence of the inmate culture and to the enormous amount of research that could be done in the prison setting. In the ensuing 40 years, many capable researchers have contributed to the still growing body of literature on the subject. The purpose of this chapter is to introduce the reader to the general pattern of that research by discussing the work and the concepts of a few key contributors. Although regretting that some important contributions are neglected in this cursory glance, we hope that it will inspire the reader to conduct his own search through a fascinating body of literature.

Formal recognition of the inmate culture stems from the efforts of Clemmer while he was a staff member in an Illinois state prison. If one follows the Mississippi River south from St. Louis, he will find Menard State Prison at the foot of the Menard Bridge on the Illinois side of the river. If by chance the traveler should visit the imposing old fortress, he might be given a booklet that has, among other things, this appropriate description of the setting for the original research into the nature of the inmate culture.

> The prison nestles in a niche in the bluffs where the Mississippi bends near Chester. The bluffs box it in, and they serve as natural walls for the institution. The rock faces have been blasted away until they are square and tall, and they guard the southern and eastern extremities of the prison proper.
>
> This—combined with the fact that the Mississippi flows in silent quest at the prison's front doors—makes the penitentiary seem almost like an island posed in a sea of silence. Something apart

from men—foreign to the rest of the world—is the feeling one gets when he approaches the main entrance.

In a way this is right—because it was intended that way in the beginning.[1]

CLEMMER—PRISON COMMUNITY

Clemmer's *The Prison Community*[2] is the acknowledged classic of the inmate culture literature. For reasons not known to us, Clemmer elected to disguise the location of his research; his book does not name the prison where his research was accomplished nor does he so much as reveal the name of the state in which the prison is located. Nonetheless, he does describe the characteristics of the geographical area from which the inmates are drawn (unmistakably Southern Illinois) and the features of the prison (unquestionably Menard State Prison). The academic community of Southern Illinois pays tribute to Clemmer's influence by proudly pointing out to criminology students that Clemmer was once the staff sociologist at Menard.

Even the Menard inmates seem to be vaguely aware of Clemmer's efforts some forty years ago. While teaching college extension courses at Menard during the academic year of 1966-67, an inmate, during a classroom coffee break, approached us with a request that we obtain a book for him from the library at Southern Illinois University. Not knowing the name of the book or the author, he attempted to describe the nature of the book to us. In the paranoid fashion of inmates, he made it clear that the local inmate legends told of a book, written by a former staff member, which exposed the faults of the institution in a most damaging manner. This book, the inmate believed, was kept out of the institution by the officials who did not want the inmates to have access to such explosive material.

Given his expectations concerning the nature of Clemmer's work, we fear that my inmate friend would have been grossly disappointed if we had provided the book. The book, contrary to his expectations, is not an exposé of prison conditions written by an intense prison reformer; such books have existed since man conceived of the idea of using incarceration as punishment, and even before that when prisons were used to hold the prisoner until he could be punished.

Perhaps the anecdote about the Menard inmate is helpful in explaining the nature of the fresh approach to prison literature that Clemmer originated. Prior to his research, prison literature focused on the pro and con arguments about using long term incarceration as a method of dealing with the offender. While reformers pointed out the horrors of prison life and the changes that were needed, other writers insisted that long term incarceration was an improvement over the older form of dealing with the offender which involved generous application of banishment and corporal or capital punishment.

As a sociologist, Clemmer, accepted the *reality* of long term incarceration and studied inmates to determine the *effects* of long term imprisonment. Without dissipating his energies in deploring the status quo, he studied the system as he found it. As Clemmer's studies progressed during the early 1930s, he realized that long term incarceration creates a unique set of social conditions: a relatively large number of individuals are forced to live a regimented life in close proximity year after year. The individuals have in common the fact that they are all of the same sex and the fact that they all have been convicted of a felony; otherwise, the group is heterogenous in that the individuals vary greatly in age, intelligence, occupation, ethnic background, education, physical condition, attitudes, and so on.

Clemmer's sociological training apparently led him to view the collection of inmates as a society unto itself. Even though most of the individuals were a part of it for a relatively short period, the prison community existed within the walls of the prison for decade after decade. If prisoners formed a community, reasoned Clemmer, then that community must have a culture, which would include a body of knowledge, art, law, beliefs, customs, and any other habits gained by man as a part of society.[3] Continuing, Clemmer pointed out that prison inmates are a community and that a community has a culture that determines the behavior patterns of the individuals involved. Behavior is determined by social relationships; in turn, social relationships are formulated within the framework of a culture. An individual will behave in a manner prescribed by the culture of which he is a part. If the prison culture differs from the culture of the free world, the inmate will behave differently inside the prison than he would behave outside. Furthermore, participation in the inmate culture for a number of years could have a long-lasting impact on the individual by making it difficult for him to adjust to the cultural norms of the outside world when he leaves the institution.

Having concluded that a prison population is a community with a distinct culture, Clemmer proceeded to study that culture largely by concentrating upon prison argot. The logic of proceeding in this manner is that language transmits much of that which we know as culture.[4] As with many types of groups who have special words for things of interest, prisoners also have a distinctive language of their own in the form of slang terms. Clemmer lists some 383 argot terms he found to be commonly known to the majority of inmates in Menard.[5] For instance; a "fish" is "one newly arrived in prison," and a "kite" is "an illicit note or letter passed between inmates." Sixty percent of the terms that he compiled referred directly to crime and to prisons.[6] In studying Clemmer's "dictionary," it was surprising to find that we had heard Menard inmates use many of the same argot phrases even though we worked among the inmates some 27 years after Clemmer's book was published. Even more revealing is the fact that much of the same special vocabulary used in Menard is used in prisons throughout the United States.

After Clemmer had a well-formulated concept of the prison community and a strategy for studying the structure of such a community, he proceeded to carefully analyze the nature of the social groups as they formed in the prison community, the leadership role as it developed in those groups, the nature of social controls, sexual patterns within the community, and a number of other relationships within the framework of his concept of the prison community. Although it is not our intention to attempt to summarize his conclusions, it does seem desirable to note the significance and durability of Clemmer's work. He confirmed the existence of an inmate culture and convinced his contemporaries that it was a significant facet of the correctional discipline—an aspect worthy of continued study and development. Clemmer established the basic technique of studying the inmates' social relationships largely through prison argot. In addition, his influence remains with us in contemporary inmate culture literature in that our contemporaries follow Clemmer's technique of giving examples of colorful inmate conversations and anecdotes interspersed with more prosaic stretches of formal theory.

SYKES—INMATES RUN PRISONS

Gresham M. Sykes is a second early pioneer in inmate culture studies. His book, *The Society of Captives*,[7] is no less a penological classic than Clemmer's *The Prison Community*. Unlike Clemmer, Sykes begins his book by identifying the setting of his research as the New Jersey State Maximum Security Prison at Trenton.[8] Of course, it is not possible to gauge the impact of a particular book, but some significance can be attached to the fact that the book is still in print, although it was originally published in 1958 by Princeton University Press.[9] We suspect that it has been more widely read than Clemmer's book because of Sykes's delightful writing style and brevity.

Sykes's work is especially helpful in understanding the impact of the inmate culture on the operation of the prison. Penologists are fond of saying that the inmates run the prisons. That phrase has several meanings. It could on one hand mean that inmates perform most of the household chores of an institution and do a major portion of the clerical work; on the other hand, saying that the inmates run the prison can also refer to the power of the inmate culture—community strength which gives the inmate a degree of autonomy and control over the daily life of the penitentiary. Sykes clarifies the nature of inmate control by analyzing "the defects of total power"[10] in the prison environment.

Prison guards, he points out, are in an arkward position in attempting to exercise control over inmates. The guard cannot often resort to the application of force in order to maintain discipline because it is not practical for a guard, armed only with a club, to attack a group of potentially violent prisoners. In addition, the consequences of his doing so could bring disciplinary action against him from his superiors, even if he escapes instant retaliation by the inmates. Knowing that his superiors will begin to note that he has difficulty in doing his job, the guard is hesitant to bring frequent formal written charges against inmates. For the guard to resort to coercion is a sign of inefficiency that may ultimately cause him to lose his job. The question posed and answered by Sykes is simply: By what means does the guard control the inmate? It is clear that the guard's ability to act as a custodian is not based on power;[11] rather, the guard's ability to function is based largely upon the cooperation that he can obtain from the inmates through the use of informal social controls. More specifically, Sykes argues that "reciprocity" is the key weapon in the guard's arsenal.[12]

Perceiving that he must win a degree of acceptance from the inmates, the guard does this by distributing the limited range of rewards that he has to offer. The rewards available for distribution are few because the prisoner receives almost all of his privileges noncontingently when he enters the prison. Thus the guard is left with only the coercive technique of withdrawing privileges as a formal means of control. Informal means developed by guards involve rewarding the prisoners for general adherence to major institution rules by overlooking their minor violations such as cooking in cells and stealing sugar from the dining hall. That is to say; the guard is willing to overlook some rule infractions deliberately, and the inmates are willing to reciprocate by letting the guard control them in a general way.

Sykes's clarification of the relationship existing between the guard and the inmate is particularly helpful in understanding the operation of the sub rosa economic system as it will be explained later. The activity in the sub rosa system is frequently on a rather large scale. The guards could not be expected to be gullible, nor are they totally blind to the continual presence of illicit activity and contraband; rather, they actually tolerate a significant amount of such activity.

Sykes's research is also an excellent source to study in order to begin to understand the complex wants and needs of inmates. A good deal of the economic activity described in later chapters seems bizarre unless one has some insight into the nature of the deprivation imposed upon inmates by their imprisonment. The basic economic condition of the inmate can only be described as poverty. Yet the inmate's poverty is of a special kind, for poverty generally implies a struggle to obtain a subsistence level of food, clothing, and shelter. In the case of the inmate, the institution provides food, clothing, and shelter. Sykes explains the essential elements of inmate deprivation partially in terms of inmate desire for a greater variety, quality, and quantity of goods and services. However, the inmate is deprived in other important ways too: he is deprived of heterosexual relationships, autonomy, and security.[13] Deprivations such as these give rise to demand for peculiar types of goods and services that serve a number of purposes.

Another important type of correctional research done by sociologists is the construction of typologies. In broad terms, typologies are ". . . the classification and explanation of specific *patterns of criminal behavior* in terms of the particular kinds of offenders who engage in these specific patterns of crime."[14] In the inmate culture literature, typologies take on a slightly different posture owing to the fact that researchers are attempting to group inmates into patterns of behavior that are identifiable as distinct facets of the inmate culture. Inmates take on certain roles, and the inmate culture defines the role expectations so that, to a limited extent, the observer can predict the reaction of an inmate to given social situations.

Sykes's *The Society of Captives* has an intriguing development of inmate typologies in terms of "argot roles."[15] Instead of devising formal names for observable patterns of inmate behavior, Sykes simply uses the slang names already being used by inmates. Of course, the existence of these argot terms indicates that the inmates themselves are capable of recognizing and identifying the behavior patterns and the corresponding responses to given social situations in prison. To briefly illustrate the nature of these argot roles used by Sykes (and others) a few of the classic roles will be discussed: the "rat," "center man," "gorilla," "merchant," "punk," and "wolf." No one could say that prisoners do not use descriptive titles.

The "rat" is the prisoner who betrays his colleagues by allowing information to flow across forbidden communication barriers (generally, this means giving information to the guards).[16] The application of the term "rat" to a prisoner invokes a vivid concept of the kind of behavior expected of that inmate and the kinds of attitudes that other inmates will have toward him. One can, if he so desires, add layers of complexity to the basic identification of the "rat" role. For example, Elmer H. Johnson identifies six rat subtypes: quislings, cornered rats, accommodated rats, unsocialized, mentally maladjusted, and flaccid rats.[17]

Sykes identifies a type that he calls a "center man." The inmate who assumes this role identifies with the value system of his keepers rather than accepting the value system of the inmate culture. The center man (the same type is known as a "square john" in other institutions) rejects the inmate culture because he sincerely believes the values of the free society are superior to those of the inmate culture.[18]

The "gorilla" role applies to the inmate who attempts to alleviate his poverty by taking the goods and services he desires from other inmates. The inmate who plays this role need not necessarily be the biggest and strongest man in the cellblock; however, he must be willing to apply force by using a weapon such as a homemade knife or a club. Sykes notes in passing that the relatively large number of inmates playing the gorilla role in prisons accounts for the demand for the manufacture of primitive weapons within the inmate culture.[19]

One of the more important roles for the purposes of this book is the "merchant" or "peddlar" type. The merchant is the entrepreneur in the inmate culture—the man who organizes, finances, and conducts the various activities of the sub rosa economic system. Within the value system of the inmate culture, he is seen as profiting from the dilemma of his fellow prisoners.[20] In later chapters, we shall refer to this type of role rather extensively.

Sykes identifies an array of argot roles that center around the homosexual activity in male prisons. This material is vital for the novice correctional practitioner who needs to be able to understand the social meanings of homosexuality in prisons. As we noted before, sexual deprivation is a part of the poverty enforced upon the inmate by his keepers. Owing to the absence of opportunities for heterosexual relationships, homosexual activity appears to be somewhat more pervasive inside the walls than it is on the street. Even so, inmates meticulously attempt to distinguish between "true" homosexuality and homosexuality which is either expedient or unavoidable. Homosexuality is "unavoidable" in the case of the "weak" inmate who allows himself to be forced into a feminine role; Sykes identifies this type as the "punk." Homosexuality is classed as "expedient" in the case of the aggresive inmate, called a "wolf," who participates in sexual activities only in the male role and at his own option. The "real" homosexual participates because it is his preference whether he is incarcerated or not. The argot role of the real homosexual is termed a "fag" on the east coast or a "queen" on the west coast.[21]

There exists also a role designation for the irrational inmate who continually disturbs the peace of the institution through his futile revolt against the guards. In the institution which Sykes studied, these men were known as "ball busters" and were considered by other inmates to be disruptive influences in the orderly activity of the prison.[22] The inmate who is easily aroused by actions of other inmates (as opposed to actions of guards) has his own label, he is the "tough."[23] The chief characteristic of the tough is that he is willing to fight any inmate, large or small. The "hipster," a different type, adopts the mannerism of the tough but he is putting on a false front.[24]

The argot roles that have been identified thus far are, to some extent, descriptive of behavior patterns that represent degrees of deviation from the norms of the inmate culture. The inmate who lives up to the expectations—the norms of behavior—of the inmate culture is the "real man."[25] The real man is an inmate leader in the sense that he is admired and respected by other inmates who support the values of the inmate culture. These argot roles have picturesque names that reveal, to a fair degree, the attitudes of the inmates toward those roles. Through analysis of argot roles and the sets of role behavior expectations that accompany them, Sykes was able to isolate the key elements of the inmate code.

To complete our summary of Sykes's contribution, and to shed additional light on the nature of the argot roles, we must briefly note his conclusions on the inmate value system. The explicit identification of the chief tenents of the inmate code was published a few years after the appearance of *The Society of Captives.* Sykes, in collaboration with Sheldon L. Messinger in 1960, precisely delineated these tenets in *Theoretical Studies in Social Organization of the Prison.*[26] In summary form, these tenets are: (1) loyalty to other convicts in presenting a united front against the administration; (2) staying cool by playing down feuds and grudges; (3) avoiding any form of exploitation of other inmates; (4) being tough and individualistic; and (5) avoidance of according any prestige or respect to the custodians.[27] By studying the tenets of the inmate code in relation to the argot rules previously described, the pecking order that exists within the confines of the inmate culture can be roughly distinguished.

SCHRAG—SQUARE JOHNS AND RIGHT GUYS

Clarence Schrag maintains that the inmate social roles set up a system of mutual care and protection. The mutual obligations created within the inmate culture strengthen inmate morale and, more significantly, protect inmates engaged in illicit activities. Protection is necessary, not only from staff members but also from inmates who are not participating in the illegal activities. Schrag feels that the strongest tenet in the inmate code of behavior is the rule that one inmate must not interfere with another inmate's participation in illicit activity.[28]

Schrag's purpose in this research was to attempt to relate the social types in some theoretical framework. He does this by using role configurations—the empirical regularities that exist among role alternatives. He believes that alternatives surrounding a focal issue are empirically connected with alternatives around a different issue;[29] in other words, the action of a given social type is predictable. Proceeding to study role configurations that cut across a number of focal issues, Schrag developed four configurations that met his criteria. He identifies the social types in terms of their argot roles (square john, right guy, con politician, and outlaw), but prefers to use different, more neutral, terminology (prosocial, antisocial, pseudosocial, and asocial) in further development of the characteristics.[30] Table 2-1 shows the relationships among Schrag's terms in the first and second column and, insofar as possible, the argot roles identified by Sykes. The third column is our attempt to compare Sykes's terms with Schrag's labels in order to relate their contributions.

Schrag's major findings concerning the social types identified in Table 2-1 indicate that their attitudes, social experiences and crimes differed in distinct ways. For example, he found that prosocial inmates frequently are

Table 2-1. Comparison of Terms Designating Social Types

Argot Term Noted by Schrag	Label Assigned by Schrag	Label in Sykes's Identification of Argot Roles
Square john	Prosocial	Center man
Right guy	Antisocial	Real man
Con politician	Pseudosocial	(not identified)
Outlaw	Asocial	Ball buster

convicted of crimes of passion—a violent crime against a person that involves a flash of temper or emotion. Some prosocial inmates have been convicted of a naive property crime, such as forging a check in one's home town.[31] These offenses are "situational" in that they are a once-in-a-lifetime occurrence due to intense emotional pressure. Having the same value systems as their custodians, prosocial inmates sympathize with prison officials and maintain close contact with their friends and business associates on the outside while they are in prison.[32]

The "right guy" or antisocial inmate displays a strikingly different pattern not only in his social background but also in the types of crimes for which he is convicted. Schrag found that he typically had a career of many arrests, initially for juvenile type thefts, later advancing to unsophisticated crimes—those for which little skill is required as in robbery, burglary, and assault.[33] The records on the social background of the antisocial inmate show that he is often from urban slum areas and has earned his living by performing minor duties for organized crime. Rebellion against the generally accepted norms of society is a pattern in his life style.[34] The prison life of the antisocial inmate follows the same general model inasmuch as he continues to identify with the criminal element and to rebel against established authority.[35]

Schrag's assessment of the "con politician" or pseudosocial inmate shows that he comes from a middle class family background (generally a family that had some disharmony) and achieved a degree of respectability before getting involved with crime. Being a bit better educated and slightly more intelligent than the antisocial offender, his crimes are of the more sophisticated variety, including embezzlement and fraud.[36] Pseudosocial inmates exploit the social conditions of the prison to their own advantage. They express allegiance to the prison officials when it is convenient to do so, but shift their loyalty to the inmate culture if that suits their purpose.[37]

The "outlaw" or asocial inmate in Schrag's formulation displays a pattern of irrational and bizzare behavior in committing a variety of crimes against persons and property. Apparently because he has been reared in institutions or foster homes, this offender lacks social skills. He seems unable to form personal relationships or to plan and organize his life. When incarcerated, the asocial offender becomes the prison troublemaker who engages in futile and disruptive rebellion at any opportunity.[38]

Schrag's research helps one to understand that there is a rationale behind the selection of specific roles within the inmate culture. The identification of the behavior patterns of the prosocial inmate, the antisocial inmate, the pseudosocial inmate and the asocial type, both within the prison and in terms of preinstitution experiences, gives insight into the social forces which divert a particular inmate into one role or another.

IRWIN—DOING TIME, JAILING, AND GLEANING

Providing a slightly different view of prison roles, John Irwin is also helpful in understanding the development of the prison sub rosa economic system. Irwin reasons that each inmate is faced with the problem of how to adapt to prison life, or in other words, the specific way that he will spend his time in the institution. In developing his concepts, Irwin describes some "prison-adaptive modes" used by inmates to cope with prison life. He portrays these modes as: (1) doing time, (2) jailing, (3) gleaning, and (4) disorganized criminal.[39]

The "doing time" mode of adaptation to prison life is a pragmatic approach: the convict sees his prison sentence as something to be dealt with in an expedient manner so he can return to life on the streets. Irwin gives the specific techniques by which these inmates hope to accomplish this.

> They come to prison and "do their time." They attempt to pass through this experience with the least amount of suffering and the greatest amount of comfort. They (1) avoid trouble, (2) find activities which occupy their time, (3) secure a few luxuries, (4) with the exception of a few complete isolates, form friendships with small groups of other convicts, and (5) do what they think is necessary to get out as soon as possible.[40]

Irwin notes that the "doing time" inmate believes that his goals can best be accomplished by adhering to the tenets of the inmate code. The values of the code give the time-doer some access to the friendship possibilities in the prison social life if he desires friendship; or, if he desires to be left alone, that wish will generally be respected. He also can obtain some goods and services through the sub rosa economic system if he desires luxuries that are not otherwise obtainable.

"Jailing" is a mode of adaptation which makes " . . . a world out of prison."[41] Irwin believes that jailing is characteristic of young men who have been raised in institutions:

The prison world is the only world with which he is familiar. He was raised in a world where "punks" and "queens" have replaced women, "bonaroos" are the only fashionable clothing, and cigarettes are money. This is a world where disputes are settled with a pipe or a knife, and the individual must form tight cliques for protection. His senses are attuned to iron doors banging, locks turning, shakedowns, and long lines of blue-clad convicts. He knows how to survive, in fact prosper, in this world.[42]

The inmate who is jailing is more inclined to take part in the illicit economic activity of the prison society and to become an inmate entrepreneur. In the California prison system studied by Irwin, this is known as "wheeling and dealing."[43] Obviously, the inmate who takes an entrepreneurial role is in more danger of running afoul of the prison authorities than the doing time prisoner who is satisfied to be a consumer in the system. The manufacture and trafficking of contraband items involves more risk and exposure than the mere purchase and consumption of contraband.

"Gleaning" describes the behavior of the inmate who, for one reason or another, decides to use his prison time to change his life style. He goes about improving himself by participation in the many programs made available by the treatment staff of the prison; he can acquire academic or vocational training, get cosmetic medical treatment, improve his body through sports, and so on. These activities occupy his time and give him a different orientation to life which may ultimately weaken his link to the inmate culture.[44]

The "disorganized criminal" is "human putty in the prison social world,"[45] according to Irwin. Because he is unable to plan his actions in prison, he differs from the three other types mentioned. Lacking the ability or determination to plan his adaptation mode, he may randomly fall into any of the other three patterns for no better reason than the fact that his cellmate has adopted a particular pattern[46]—Joe is doing time so he will do time.

Irwin's work indicates on one hand that a goodly number of inmates sentenced to prison make rational decisions about the pattern of adaptation that they will employ in dealing with the reality of prison life. However, an adaptive mode may appear feasible to a prisoner in one stage of his life, while another mode will seem more attractive at another time. On the other hand, the prisoner's preinstitution experiences will largely determine the adaptive mode that he perceives to be desirable. It is clear from Irwin's studies, when comparing them with earlier work done in the field, that there are several types of roles within each adaptive mode. Schrag's work had already indicated that an inmate would select a particular role partially because of his preinstitution background.

Thus, from an examination of the research of both Schrag and Irwin, a possible conclusion is that an inmate's preinstitution experiences largely determine his choice among the general adaptive modes to prison life and also determine his choice of a role alternative *within* his selected adaptive mode. Sykes's earlier studies explain the nature of the particular argot roles and Clemmer's pioneering efforts help one to understand how a prison culture arises to shape the framework of social roles.

Thus far, the social nature of women's prisons has been ignored. Since the inmate culture in women's prisons differs in a number of ways from that in male prisons, it is easier to deal with the female subculture separately. The literature that we have been describing involves empirical observations of research-minded professionals associated with institutions. Since male and female prisoners are segregated in separate institutions, it is natural that different researchers would study female institutions. Furthermore, the literature on the male inmate culture was fairly well formulated before studies of the inmate culture in women's prisons were initiated. At this point we will note two significant studies of the inmate culture in the female prison population.

WARD AND KASSEBAUM—HOMOSEXUALS AND SNITCHERS

David A. Ward and Gene G. Kassebaum wrote *Women's Prison: Sex and Social Structure* specifically as a comparison of the social nature of the women's prison with the male inmate culture already described by Clemmer, Sykes, and others.[47] While their research was not originally intended to be focused upon homosexual behavior, once the study got under way they concluded that the social structure of women's prisons is built around homosexual roles to the exclusion of practically everything else.[48]

The particular setting of the Ward and Kassebaum effort is the California Institution for Women at Frontera, a relatively large prison as compared to other institutions for female offenders (average population in 1971 was 739).[49] Ward and Kassebaum's book differs from the publications previously mentioned in an important way; they did not develop their empirical data through years of working in the prison and observing the inmates. Rather, they went to the prison as researchers, used the standard research tools available to social scientists, completed the project, and left the prison setting. However, their notes on the methodology employed indicate that the study was accomplished in scientifically acceptable fashion.[50]

When trying to determine the degree to which female prisoners adhere to the type of prisoner's code that is so evident in the male institutions, Ward and Kassebaum found some key differences. The female prisoners did place some emphasis on the desirability of not ratting on other inmates, but estimates of the proportion of the population that violated this canon ranged up to 90 percent. The female prisoner who did not "snitch" (the female term for ratting) did have status in the informal social system; she was known as a "regular." Her high status in the female inmate culture derived largely from her ability to avoid this common pitfall.[51] In any case, snitching was common enough so that it did not invoke the serious physical or sociological retaliation ordinarily found in male prisons.

In general, the female inmates at Frontera did not express a strong belief in the inmate code as it is described in male prisons, nor did they develop strong group solidarity.[52] For purposes of development of the nature of sub rosa economic systems in the inmate culture, it is interesting to note the lack of entrepreneurial effort at Frontera, partially due to the fact that incarcerated women are allowed more personal things, but, according to Ward and Kassebaum, "it is also based on the inability to organize illicit merchandising of goods due to the abundance of inmate informers."[53]

The social system existing in female prisons must be explained in almost wholly different terms. In Ward and Kassebaum's experience, any direct comparison between the male and female informal systems seems unprofitable because the only comparable roles were "the roles which deny support to the inmate code—the snitch and the related center man role type, and the square john or prosocial type of prisoner."[54] The factors which must be used to explain the informal social system in women's prisons, in view of Ward and Kassebaum, are the particular form of deprivation which incarceration imposes upon the female, the preinstitution involvement in criminal activity, and the "latent roles and latent identities prisoners bring to prison with them."[55]

Previous studies on the nature of the criminal culture in male institutions make it relatively clear that the prisoners, to some extent, bring to prison with them a set of antiestablishment norms which they have assimilated in delinquent subcultures on the streets. This seems to be true in the case of women prisoners as well, but Ward and Kassebaum point out that women bring to prison a set of norms which they have obtained by virtue of their sex-related roles in American society.[56] That is to say, discrimination against women in the American society has limited and specified the types of social roles that a woman can play and this becomes the frame of reference women bring to prison, along with any additional norms they may have picked up from delinquent subcultures. To a large extent, women, being habituated to roles within the social mechanism of the family, use the family as a point of reference for social organization. This is reflected in Ward and Kassebaum's conclusions, as follows.

> Men come to prison as husbands and fathers but more importantly as breadwinners—the principal determiners of the social status of the family. Their self-definitions give greater emphasis to their occupational roles . . . .
> Women prisoners suffer more from separation from families and disruptions of familial roles. Women bring to prison with them

identities and self-conceptions which are based principally on familial roles as wives, mothers, and daughters, and their related roles (fiancees and girl friends). These differences reflect the division of labor in kinship systems which place on women the principal responsibilities of housekeeping and care of children.[57]

Given a proper understanding of the family role orientation of female prisoners, it is less difficult to come to understand the social significance of female homosexuality in prison. Homosexual roles are intended to make prison life endurable, to provide interpersonal relationships that approximate the familiar family roles—thus homosexuality becomes a mode of adaptation to prison life for women. Ward and Kassebaum illustrate how this is encouraged through folklore and aphorisms saying, " 'You can't make it unless you have someone!' " and " 'Everyone is doing it so if you don't you are either a prude or crazy.' "[58]

The findings and conclusions of Ward and Kassebaum have been confirmed and enriched by an independent study being conducted at roughly the same time in a federal reformatory. Let us turn our attention to that particular research.

GIALLOMBARDO—MOTHER AND FAMILY

Rose Giallombardo's research culminated in a comprehensive book called *The Society of Women: A Study of a Women's Prison,*[59] a study of the informal social system in the Federal Reformatory for Women at Alderson, West Virginia, built in 1927 to hold a normal capacity of 475, but in 1970 averaging 525.[60] Alderson inmates, according to Giallombardo, were organized around families. Her work, though done independently of that of Ward and Kassebaum, stresses some of the same factors: (1) that the informal social structure of women's prisons differs significantly from that of male prisons; (2) that the social roles in the female inmate culture focus upon homosexual relations as a mode of adaptation to prison life; and (3) that the mode of adaptation is best understood by assessing the preinstitution experiences of female offenders.

Giallombardo proposes that the real basis and purpose of homosexual relations in the female prison is the mechanism that it provides for creating a social structure—a type of social structure familiar to women because of the sex-related roles imposed upon them by outside society. Being the form of social organization that is familiar to women on the outside, the family becomes the form that is used to organize social relationships on the inside. The basic unit, then, is the homosexual marriage, which defines not only a husband-wife type of interpersonal relationship but is also used as a reference point to establish other kinship relationships that become quite extensive and include mothers, fathers, sons, daughters, brothers, sisters, uncles, nephews, aunts, nieces, and so on.[61] The social organization function of these roles is explained by Giallombardo as follows.

> The prison homosexual marriage alliance and the larger informal family groupings provide structures wherein the female inmate's needs may find fulfillment and expression during the period of incarceration. Kinship and marriage ties make it possible for the inmates to ascribe and achieve social statuses and personalities in the prison other than that of inmate which are consistent with the cultural expectations of the female role in American society.[62]

In later chapters we will again refer to Giallombardo's research and, in fact, to the works of all the authors discussed in this chapter, as their research is used to aid in analysis of the sub rosa economic system in prisons. Before proceeding to the discussion of economic events in the inmate culture, we wish to note the work of one other person in relation to the subject matter at hand. The work that we have discussed thus far involves research and writing done by persons who are academic sociologists. Since in some cases their efforts are on a highly theoretical plane, it is not always immediately obvious what implications, if any, their discussions have for the world of the correctional practitioner and the plight of the inmate. We wish to illustrate briefly some of the results of this type of research in terms of its impact upon the career and work style of the warden of a state prison for male felons.

WATKINS—MOVE THE SOLID

John C. Watkins was, for more than a decade, the warden of Draper Correctional Center—a 600-inmate-capacity, medium security prison for males in rural Alabama. He is by profession and inclination a practitioner of penology rather than an academician. His college training for entry into the criminal justice field was, as is typical, an interdisciplinary type of curriculum. While he is not highly specialized in any one academic discipline, he has the basics of a number of subject areas within the social sciences and is able to select whatever social science concept or concepts he deems to be appropriate to help solve the everyday tasks of penology. Watkins was exposed to the literature of the inmate culture, along with other frames of reference outside academic sociology, during his preparation for his career.

He came to realize that Draper had a strong inmate culture that effectively cut off communication between the inmates and the staff, acting as a barrier to any rehabilitation efforts that might be attempted. In 1962 he decided that he would systematically study the Draper inmate culture as the main element in his strategy to achieve the rehabilitation goals of the prison.

Believing that since the inmate culture acted to solidify inmate opposition to staff values, the first logical step in a rehabilitation effort was to gain an understanding of the inner workings of the culture in his prison in order to control and change it.[63] Warden Watkins found that his prison *did* have the social types described in the literature and that the convict code did have a strong influence on the behavior of his inmates. The code protected the inmate culture against rats and center men types who posed a threat to the goals of the inmate culture. The inmates, indeed, had a strong belief that grave consequences would befall any rat or center man—a more prominent expression of this viewpoint was the saying that, "If you tell, you will get your head torn up."[64]

Having established the existence and the approximate degree of influence of the inmate culture, Warden Watkins and his staff decided that for operational purposes they could classify all the prisoners according to their relationship to the inmate culture. Their operational classification is shown in Table 2-2.[65] The first column divides the prison population into two broad categories—inmates who are not affected by the inmate code and inmates who are influenced by it. The right-hand column is our own attempt to correlate the Draper terminology with those terms previously discussed in other inmate culture literature and mentioned above.

The first broad category, prosocial-type inmates, can identify with the rehabilitation goals of the prison because, coming to prison as a result of a "situational" offense, they never attached themselves to the

Table 2-2. Operational Classification of Draper Population

Categories	*Equivalent Type*
Inmate (free from influence of convict code)	Square John Center Man (prosocial)
Convict (influenced by convict code)	—
☐ Adapter (fears the convict code)	Con Politician (pseudosocial)
☐ Character defect (not committed to any code)	Ball Buster Outlaw (asocial)
☐ Solid convict (upholds convict code)	Real Man Right Guy (antisocial)

tenets of the inmate code, or because they changed their alliegance from the inmate culture to the values of the staff (and the outside society). The "adapter," "character defect," and "solid convict" are representatives of several social types who adhere to the inmate code in various degrees for different reasons. Adapters have no deep-seated attachment to the code, but they feel that it is expedient to pretend to believe in it so long as it is strong. The character defect type also finds it convenient to live by the code, but he too has little belief in it, or in any other social scheme for that matter, and will betray the code when he can profit from doing so. The solids are the upholders and managers of the code those convict leaders who are firmly committed to the tenets of the inmate code.[66]

Warden Watkins's strategy was a concept that is simple as a principle but extraordinarily difficult to put into practice; he decided to intervene in the system to weaken the power of the inmate code. The strategy was to decrease the size of the convict group by transferring its disciples to the inmate or prosocial group. Inmates were less likely to become recidivists than were convicts.

In order to accomplish his objectives, Warden Watkins decided to work with the solids, because, if a solid could be converted to a prosocial type, his clique would possibly follow him into the different frame of reference. As more solids were converted, the power of the inmate code would gradually diminish and, when its strength wained, those prisoners who subscribed to its tenets only out of fear would no longer support it.

Watkins studied the social and criminal backgrounds of the solids that he could identify in his prison population. As Schrag had pointed out in his research, these antisocial men had a number of pre-institution experiences in common. Clearly identifying the characteristics of the antisocial convict, Watkins found that

> They got into trouble early in life; came from female-dominated, fatherless homes, and had intense boy-gang and other institutional and criminal experiences. Almost to a man, they are tattooed. They have their own religion: "Thou shall not tell." Everything else is permitted, but they are very moral in their loyalty to the system. If you ask one of them to tell you something, he often puts his hand over his heart and says, "I know it will help me to tell you, but if I did I couldn't live with myself, I could not look into a mirror or hold my head up."[67] . . .
>
> Almost all solid convicts come from fatherless homes, which are dominated by females. From this type of home, especially if it is from a lower income group, many boys escape "Momma" and find their maleness in the anti-social, anti-authority, aggressive boy-gang. A boy with this background embraces his group with great intensity, and takes on its value system to the exclusion of all

others. He learns to carry on various kinds of criminal activities. Inevitably, he is arrested and convicted. And usually, while in jail, he takes on the final overt markings of the criminal subculture—the tattoos. He is now ready to live in the institution as one of the elite—a solid convict.[68]

While developing his techniques for intervening in the criminal culture, Watkins became aware that the process involves several salient features. For conceptual purposes we have labeled the key features or four steps of his technique in Table 2-3.[69]

The first step noted in Table 2-3 is the identification of the solid convicts. This is more complex than it would appear to be because the solid, who is easily mistaken for a character defect, operates quietly in the background. The difficulty of correctly identifying solids makes verification of the identification an important step. Both selection and verification involve careful observation, background studies, questioning, and staff consultations over a period of time.[70]

Converting the solid to a prosocial stance, is, of course, a formidable and involved process. The steps listed in Table 2-3 under "conversion to prosocial type" are general guidelines provided by Watkins. He maintains that an initial approach to dealing with a particular solid is to disturb his position or equilibrium in the system by instituting some change that will throw him off balance and make him vulnerable or more susceptible to attitude change. Techniques such as curtailment of the solid's activities, changing his sleeping quarters or job, and intensifying the degree of custodial control exercised over him all increase the inmate's vulnerability.[71]

Revelation, the next step, is simply a forthright explanation of the sociological determinants of the solid's behavior. For example, the warden

Table 2-3. Watkins's Intervention Technique

1. Identification of solids
2. Verification of identification
3. Conversion to prosocial type

    ☐ Curtailment of power
    ☐ Revelation
    ☐ Significant other relationship
    ☐ Identity change

4. Followup

would explain to the solid why he became involved in boy-gang activity as a result of his particular home life, how he acquired the values of the criminal culture in his boy-gang associations, how these values caused him to be convicted for a crime (or a number of crimes) and, finally, the certainty that he will continue to return to prison unless he changes.[72] One would not expect that the logic of the lecture would sway the solid, but it does indicate to him that the staff member knows a good deal more about him than he suspected, and it also tells him that the staff member has a personal interest in him—that the staff member is not his enemy.[73]

Watkins has demonstrated that gradually the solid can be drawn away from the convict culture. No matter how small, each step away from the values of the inmate culture is reinforced by rewarding the solid with some privilege that he would deem desirable. However, the solid is not allowed to manipulate the staff member. Rather, the staff member gradually becomes a significant other or "father figure" for the solid.[74] The inmate is building new relationships.

Ultimately, the solid changes his identity, determines to change the direction of his life and becomes prosocial. Although it is regarded as a by-product, an indication that the process is working comes when the inmate is willing to inform; informing illustrates a definitive break with the values of the convict code.[75] The inmate, having changed his value system, begins the adaptation mode of "gleaning" described by Irwin. It logically follows, that the "weaker" convicts can be more easily persuaded to give up the values of the convict code once a fair number of solids have done so.

This brief survey of Watkins's strategy has been posed here to demonstrate that the extraordinary and innovative practitioner such as Warden Watkins can use the knowledge of the inmate culture literature in conjunction with other social science precepts to bring about constructive change in the system. Watkins almost single-handedly destroyed the strong convict culture influence in Draper and replaced it with a treatment mileau. Unfortunately for Draper, Watkins resigned his position in 1972 and accepted another post where he no longer is in daily contact with inmates.

SUMMARY

In this chapter some of the basic findings in a few of the landmark studies on the inmate culture have been presented. We have simplified some of the concepts covered and ignored the works of several important contributors to the field, our purpose being to provide a bare skeleton of the existing theoretical framework of the inmate culture. The initial studies of the inmate culture (Clemmer and Sykes) conceptualized it almost solely as a unique form of social organization arising as a reaction to imprisonment, whereas the later studies place more emphasis upon preinstitution factors in determining the source of the convict value system. When focusing on the economic aspects of inmate culture, we will again be referring to the studies of the authors discussed in this chapter as well as to the studies of others not heretofore mentioned.

Notes to Chapter 2

1. Illinois Department of Public Safety, *Menard: Illinois State Penitentiary*, pp. 4-5.

2. Donald Clemmer, *The Prison Community,* rev. ed. (New York: Holt, Rinehart and Winston, 1958).

3. *Ibid,.* p. 85.

4. *Ibid.,* p. 88.

5. *Ibid.,* pp. 330-336.

6. *Ibid.,* pp. 89 and 332-333.

7. Gresham M. Sykes, *The Society of Captives* (Princeton, N.J: Princeton University Press, 1971).

8. *Ibid.,* p. xvi.

9. *Ibid.,* title page.

10. *Ibid.,* pp. 40-62.

11. *Ibid.,* p. 46.

12. *Ibid.,* p. 56.

13. *Ibid.,* pp. 63-83.

14. From Roebuck, Julian B., *Criminal Typology,* 1967. Courtesy of Charles C. Thomas, Publisher, Springfield, Illinois.

15. Sykes, pp. 84-108.

16. *Ibid.,* p. 87.

17. Elmer H. Johnson, "Sociology of Confinement: Assimilation and the Prison 'Rat'," *Journal of Criminal Law, Criminology and Police Science* 51 (January-February 1961): 528-533.

18. Sykes, pp. 89-90.

19. *Ibid.,* pp. 90-91.

20. *Ibid.,* pp. 93-94.

21. *Ibid.,* pp. 95-99.

22. *Ibid.,* pp. 99-100.

23. *Ibid.,* pp. 103-104.

24. *Ibid.,* pp. 104-105.

25. *Ibid.,* pp. 101-102.

26. Gresham M. Sykes and Sheldon L. Messinger, "The Inmate Social System," in *Theoretical Studies in Social Organization of the Prison,* by Richard A. Cloward and others (New York: Social Science Research Council, 1960), pp. 5-19.

27. *Ibid.,* pp. 7-10.

28. Clarence Schrag, "Some Foundations for a Theory of Correction," in *The Prison: Studies in Institutional Organization and Change,* ed. Donald R. Cressey (New York: Holt, Rinehart and Winston, 1966), pp. 309-357.

29. *Ibid.,* p. 346.

30. *Ibid.,* p. 347.

31. *Ibid.,* p. 348.

32. *Ibid.*

33. *Ibid.*
34. *Ibid.*
35. *Ibid.*
36. *Ibid.,* p. 349.
37. *Ibid.*
38. *Ibid.,* pp. 349-350.
39. John Irwin, *The Felon* (Englewood Cliffs, N.J: Prentice-Hall, 1970), pp. 67-80.
40. *Ibid.,* p. 69.
41. *Ibid.,* p. 74.
42. *Ibid.*
43. *Ibid.,* p. 75.
44. *Ibid.,* pp. 76-78.
45. *Ibid.,* p. 79.
46. *Ibid.,* p. 80.
47. David A. Ward and Gene G. Kassebaum, *Women's Prison: Sex and Social Structure* (Chicago: Aldine, 1965), p. v.
48. *Ibid.,* p. 228.
49. American Correctional Association, *Directory of Correctional Institutions and Agencies: 1971* (College Park, Md: American Correctional Association, 1972), p. 5.
50. Ward and Kassebaum, pp. 228-261.
51. *Ibid.,* p. 33.
52. *Ibid.,* p. 53.
53. *Ibid.,* p. 54.
54. *Ibid.*
55. *Ibid.,* p. 55.
56. *Ibid.,* p. 58.
57. *Ibid.,* p. 70.
58. *Ibid.,* p. 75.
59. Rose Giallombardo, *Society of Women: A Study of a Women's Prison* (New York: John Wiley, 1966).
60. American Correctional Association, p. 98.
61. Giallombardo, p. 163.
62. *Ibid.,* pp. 185-186.
63. John Cleveland Watkins, "The Modification of the Subcultures in a Correctional Institution," presented at the 94th Congress of Correction, Kansas City, Missouri, September 1, 1964, p. 1. (Mimeographed.)
64. *Ibid.,* p. 5.
65. *Ibid.,* pp. 6-8.
66. *Ibid.*
67. *Ibid.,* pp. 7-8.
68. *Ibid.,* pp. 9-10.
69. *Ibid.,* pp. 12-17.
70. *Ibid.,* pp. 13-14.
71. *Ibid.,* p. 14.
72. *Ibid.*
73. *Ibid.,* p. 15.
74. We are fortunate to be acquainted with an ex-solid personally converted and rehabilitated by Warden Watkins. On August 2, 1972, we listened to the former inmate describe the process from his perspective as he was addressing a group of probation and parole supervisors. The following day, we heard the Warden describe the process from *his* perspective while addressing the same group. It occurred to us that the process is very similar to the reality therapy form of behavior modification advocated by Dr. Glasser. See: William Glasser, *Reality Therapy: A New Approach to Psychiatry* (New York: Harper & Row, 1965).
75. Watkins, p. 15.

Chapter Three

Men's Prisons

The sub rosa economic system, which is the focus of this chapter, develops in the inmate culture of male maximum and medium custody penitentiaries. The social system in women's prisons is significantly different from that of male prisons, a point already discussed in Chapter 2; likewise the extent and nature of their economic activity is different. For this reason it is more convenient to devote the next chapter to women's prisons and this to men's. Much of the material presented here describes the economic transactions, because it is not feasible to plunge directly into analysis, implications, and conclusions until one is familiar with the patterns of production, distribution, and consumption carried on as illicit activity in American prisons. This chapter illustrates those patterns and more: the organizational techniques of prison entrepreneurs, the elaborate provisions for storage and distribution of contraband, the sub rosa monetary system and financing arrangements, and the system's response to unique demand situations.

When reading about the sub rosa system, one should be ever mindful that the conditions under which the activities occur are extremely adverse to success. Businessmen of the outside world often complain that they must operate under tough conditions: they say competition is ruthless and intense, taxes are high, and it is scarcely profitable to exploit natural resources with such stringent environmental control regulations. And when one does manage to innovate and to bid scarce resources away from competitors, then cancellation of government contracts or removal of import quotes could eliminate any potential gains. But free world businessmen enjoy help from government that provides an infrastructure (transportation, utilities, education, and public health, for example) and the general approval of society for their efforts.

Immersed in a world of restraint, inmate businessmen operate in an extremely hostile environment. Their formal government defines all their activities as illegal and imposes harsh penalties upon them if they are caught

39

engaging in their "rackets." The prison administration works along with nature to deny material resources to the sub rosa system. "Unnatural" disasters destroy their work in that prison rats inform on them and bring guards to search their hiding places for their products and means of production. Their raw materials must be stolen or converted from waste products secretly, under the watchful eyes of guards, closed circuit television cameras, and unidentified informers. They cannot devote full time to their illicit activities, but must find spare moments when they are not being marched or worked by prison personnel. While they pay no income tax as the outside businessmen know it, they may pay large amounts as "protection" to powerful inmate groups or to dishonest prison personnel. If they develop a profitable racket, competition will almost certainly arise. If they lay away savings from their profits, they must live in fear of the thieves, muggers, and murderers who are their associates and customers. Almost all this complex economic activity is conducted by men who have less than the equivalent of eight years of formal education. Under such conditions, it is a tribute to the basic ingenuity of man that any economic activity can be accomplished at all. It gives one insight into man's capacity for survival and his ability to truck and barter under near impossible circumstances.

NATURE OF PRISON POVERTY

Incarceration brings a special sort of economic pain because autonomy is lost and one's possessions are appropriated. Street clothes and shoes are taken and prison uniforms are issued—two pairs of pants and two shirts, a pair of socks and shoes, a cap, all properly stamped with a number to replace one's name. The prisoner may be given a threadbare uniform that has long since been stretched out of shape by its previous owners.

The prisoner's life is regimented: there is a period for work, an interval for sleep, an interval in the exercise yard, a time for eating, and a specified period each week for a hasty bath and shave. Heterosexual relations are obviated. Family contact is capsuled into a 2 to 3:30 Sunday afternoon visit across a table once a month. The prisoner is allowed to receive and write a few letters to a short list of approved correspondents, but it is only a matter of time before physical separation completely isolates him from outside contact.

Prison life is physical separation and isolation, but it is also psychological separation from society—rejection by society. Society no longer wants him as an honorable member because he is no longer trusted or valued. According to Gresham M. Sykes,[1] the most difficult and painful aspect of incarceration is the awareness that he is no longer trusted or morally acceptable to society. His rights of citizenship—to vote, to hold office, to sue in court—are taken away. If the inmate dwells on the affairs of the outside world, he does "hard time," but he can do "easy time" if he becomes emotionally immune and numb to the events that are a part of the outside world.

PRISONIZATION

The incarcerated, as rejected persons, simply begin to reject their keepers and the society represented by the prison officer. The free community has cast them aside so they, in turn, cast the free community aside. Once the outside world is discarded, it can no longer offend for it is no longer significant. Intially the inmate is engaged in two simultaneous processes: he is putting aside the values of the free world in his rejection of those who have seques-tered him and, at the same time, he is gradually accepting the values, customs, and general culture of the prison. These processes are called "prisoniza-tion." Through these socialization processes the inmate organization is accepted by the new inmate and thus perpetuated.

As the free community floats further and further away, the prison community takes on greater importance and meaning for the inmate. The prison community, already described, is an informal social order consisting of the numerous interrelated roles played by inmates in the system. The inmate social structure, which determines the type of status afforded an inmate, is based on the degrees to which inmates support the various components of the prison code. The code and the social system are inseparable. Becoming a member of the prison community means thinking, acting, and feeling as the community thinks, acts, and feels; it means taking on the objectives, orienta-tion, and codes of the system. The inmate social system supports group norms or a "code" that is directly related to mitigating the pains of imprisonment.[2] As meaningful connections with the free world dissolve, the prison subculture becomes more vital; in turn, as an inmate nears the end of his sentence or anticipates parole in the near future, the importance of the inmate culture dwindles.

INMATE CODE AND BUSINESS ETHICS

As has been noted in the previous chapter, the inmate code is a set of norms peculiar to the inmate world. It provides a philosophy of doing time, includes ways of implementing the maxims of the code, includes rationalizations for criminal behavior, and satisfactory solutions for obtaining illegal goods and services to mitigate the prison poverty imposed upon the inmates. Appropriate ways of dealing with officers as well as with fellow inmates are clearly stated.[3]

If the inmate code is strong in a particular prison, it unifies the inmates against the prison staff and secures coercive cooperation from detested rat and center man types who otherwise would destroy its power. The code provides a relatively safe environment for illicit economic activities. An extensive and intricate sub rosa economic system could not operate without the cooperation of the majority of the inmates; the strength of the inmate culture, functioning around a code, is the guarantee of that cooperation.

Viewed from a different perspective, the sub rosa economic system is not needed in institutions where custody plays a subordinate role to the treatment atmosphere. In institutions where treatment and rehabilitation is emphasized more than custody, the inmate maintains a greater number of contacts in the free community, is granted a greater degree of autonomy, is less regimented, and, in general, has less need for the status and autonomy that the sub rosa system can provide for him.

| The illicit economy, then, can exist only with the protection of the strong inmate culture wherein the inmates generally adhere to the values of the inmate code. It is an integral part of the inmate culture—a tool to serve the goals of the culture. It will die if the inmate culture weakens, but the inmate culture will weaken only if the rigor of confinement is mitigated to the point where the sub rosa system is no longer needed. The informal economy arises spontaneously in response to the social need of a sequestered and alienated group. When the isolation of the group is mitigated, they become a part of the larger society once more, and consequently become a part of the economic system of the larger group. |

The tenets of the inmate code preserve the unity of the inmate body. Since they constitute the value system or "morals" of the group, the tenets are necessarily the guidelines for business ethics within the group. And since the tenets have the primary goal of unifying the inmates against the staff members, they are not especially well suited as guidelines for doing business within the community.

Consider, for example, the chief tenet, which places a taboo against exploiting other inmates. Sykes and Sheldon L. Messinger found that the maxim, "don't exploit inmates" in fact sums up several maxims: "don't break your word," "don't steal from cons," "don't sell favors," "don't be a racketeer," "don't welsh on bets." They also found, in noting the characteristics an inmate must possess to be a "right guy" that it is generally expected that respectable convicts will share their amenities as gifts or favors and will not exploit other convicts by buying and selling goods that are in short supply.[4] This tenet has the practical effect of making ordinary trade for profit taboo within the culture. The existence of this tenet, which serves to unify inmates, causes an area of ambiguity within the system.

| In a capitalist economic system, profit is an appropriate reward to the entrepreneur who performs a legitimate economic function for society. Profit is not viewed as "exploitation" unless it is inordinately high or un-earned; instead, profit serves as the motivating springboard that encourages the

entrepreneur to organize the factors of production in an efficient manner. Presumably, without motivation, no entrepreneurial activity would occur; no goods and services would be forthcoming; and each individual or family would be an independent, self-subsistent unit, driven by hunger and necessity to supply their own economic needs. In such a rudimentary economy there would be no significant division of labor and no need for a monetary system. ⱶ

The inmate sub rosa economy does have a monetary system, meaningful division of labor, and a goodly amount of buying and selling for profit. The profit motive is present in the illicit economy *despite* the important taboo against selling goods in short supply. If one cursorily examined the tenets of the inmate code, one might conclude that the inmate economy could not assume the capitalist form, but rather that the inmate leader or right guy is expected to share goods in a balanced reciprocity of gifts.

The *ideal* of business ethics expressed by the inmate code is a form of Christian Socialism in terms of economic organization. Basically it calls for the demonstration of Christian principles in community life and the establishment of economic organizations that foster cooperation and profit sharing. However, one must remember that the inmate behavior code expresses an *ideal* or behavior *pres*cription and does not provide a behavior *descri*ption ₵ of actual practice.

Even so, the admonition to not exploit another inmate does have an impact on the illicit economy. The entrepreneur or "merchant" is deviant in relation to the inmate code even though he performs a vital function for the inmate culture in general. He is deviant in that his behavior is not exactly in accordance to the behavior prescription of the code. The result of his variance from the norms of the code is that he is not accorded much prestige in the system; he is, so to speak, beneath the right guy, who does not openly engage in entrepreneurial activity.

Thus, one result of the taboo of exploitation is attaching a degree of stigma to the inmate role of merchant. One is reminded of medieval Catholicism, which likewise had a taboo against trade (buying and selling for profit) to the extent that European Catholics had to import Jews to handle their trade and banking functions. They could not function adequately without the money changers, but they looked down upon them and disparaged their efforts. The money changers became wealthy, but they were without prestige in the larger community. The analogy fits the prison culture. Although the merchants command the resources of the illicit economy— sometimes even becoming wealthy by inmate standards—they cannot command great prestige and influence in the system because of the stigma of exploitation stemming from the inmate code.

Nevertheless, it is difficult, if not impossible, to be leader of fellow convicts if one has no favors to dispense to lieutenants and no wealth to buy the symbols of power. Some inmate leaders are entrepreneurs and are able to function as entrepreneurs without losing prestige because the system has an ingenious mechanism for circumventing the rule that the inmate must not exploit his fellows by selling goods in short supply. This mechanism is clearly illustrated in Schrag's description of a prison food racket. Clarence Schrag points out that food may be stolen from the prison kitchen under two sets of circumstances, with the disposition of the food depending upon the particular circumstance under which it was obtained.

One possibility for obtaining stolen food is opportunistic. For example, an inmate runner delivering a message to the prison kitchen might avail himself of the unexpected opportunity to steal a few apples in his jacket pocket. Under these circumstances, the inmate is said to "score" and the tenet against selling applies to his situation: he must consume the apples himself or share them with his friends, but it would be improper to sell them—improper according to the inmate code, that is. On the other hand, food is regularly stolen from the kitchen on a highly organized and systematic basis. These organized thefts are "routes" and not "scores." A stigma is not attached to the selling of pilfered food obtained on routes. These routes more often than not are highly organized forms of economic activity. Schrag notes that the food racket employs division of labor and responsibility with some inmates being assigned the task of obtaining food items and other inmates performing the role of distributor. Both cash and credit sales are made. [5]

Thus the inmate social system has a mechanism for circumventing an awkward tenet, and the illicit economic system need not be organized as a form of Christian Socialism, as the value system would seem to indicate. The morality of the system does provide for profit motivated activity and does allow inmate heroes to engage in entrepreneurial activity without being stigmatized. In practice, the right guy may be the inmate leader working quietly behind the scenes to organize and operate the food routes through a series of lieutenants. He receives profits from the efforts, but these are respectable profits. It is admirable to fool and exploit the keepers.

The exploitation tenet of the inmate code would seem to apply more to the disposition of his profits than their acquisition. When he uses his profits to obtain the luxuries of prison life, the code dictates that he freely shares these luxuries with his clique members. To attempt to sell these goods to his immediate friends would be reprehensible. His situation is analogous to that of the teacher in the free community who freely gives his stock in trade (knowledge) to any acquaintance who asks him for information; the teacher would be shunned if he attempted to charge the acquaintance a fee. Conversely, the teacher can receive compensation for transmitting knowledge systematically and regularly to a group of students with no stigma attached to that type of payment. While the inmate culture abhors individual greed, it rewards time utility and place utility in the systematic delivery of goods and services.

An important part of demand involves delivery of goods and services when and where they are wanted

One weakness in the existing literature on the inmate culture is the confusion surrounding the role of the merchant. He is disparaged in the literature as an exploiter of other inmates, while the right guy is viewed as an entirely separate social role—a prestige role, gained partially because he lacks the qualities of the merchant. When one attempts to apply this theoretical structure to an actual prison population, the results are confusing. The right guy and the merchant cannot be viewed as separate and distinct social roles. We conclude from our investigations that a merchant type may not necessarily have all of the qualities needed to be a right guy leader type, but, on the other hand, the right guy is not necessarily precluded from being a merchant. The right guy can engage in entrepreneurial activity without stigma if he is skillful in using the mechanism for circumventing the maxim against selling goods in short supply. He must not be blatant in his profiteering if he does not want the other inmates to perceive him as belonging in the lower status role of merchant. To sum up, a skillful inmate can obtain the financial benefits of the merchant role and the status benefits of the right guy role simultaneously.

This does not preclude a separate role designation for a less skillful merchant type who lacks the traits of a leader. Again, an example from the free community might help to clarify the issue. Visualize a medium sized city which has three major manufacturing firms. One of the firms is owned and operated by a local family. The patriarch of the family is a wealthy entrepreneur who beneficently participates in the local community life. Since his firm provides employment for many of the community members and the taxes his firm pays finances much of the local government activity, he is regarded as too powerful to offend. The image that he presents to the community is that of "community leader." He is careful to appear always as a benevolent patron of the arts and civic leader—never as merely a successful businessman. De-emphasizing his role as profit-taker, and stressing his function of generous dispenser of the fruits of his wealth and good fortune, he is a river through which good things flow unto his people. Because of his power and his skill in managing his role, the community thinks of him as a beneficent leader.

Now consider for a moment a local owner of a used car lot in the same city. Being neither powerful nor skillful in role playing or building an image, he is regarded by the community as a merchant or peddler. Both entrepreneurs perform an important social function for the community, but the used car dealer has less prestige and far less power.

In summary, the prison community has an ethical framework within which business must be conducted. A part of the morality of the framework operates to deny the awarding of much prestige to the greedy because individual avarice is believed to be detrimental to the fabric of the inmate social structure. Yet there is hypocrisy in the system, for it provides a distinct mechanism for circumventing a maxim which would work to deny wealth to its leaders. We conclude that the ethics of the economic system are such that the leader may be a merchant, but a merchant is not necessarily a leader. Previously excessively compartmentalized, these two roles cannot always be perceived as separate and distinct. The expressed ideal of the inmate code would indicate that the organization of economic activity must be predicated on a system of Christian Socialism, but the reality of the operation of the system does not support that view.

RESOURCES AVAILABLE TO THE SYSTEM

Sociologists who have studied the inmate culture have made passing references to the illicit economic system that are sometimes inaccurate. Sykes, in discussing the propensity of the gorilla social type to take goods from other inmates forcibly, notes the scarcity within the social system and says that "the society of captives cannot appreciably improve its material level of existence by wringing additional supplies from its environment, either rightfully or wrongfully."[6]

Sykes's statement is a common misconception, frequently found among the well trained, that bears careful examination. If it were true, then the illicit economic system serves no useful purpose other than to divide the few available goods among the prison population. The erroneous view being stated by Sykes is a view of resources as a given stock of materials to be divided among men and consumed. Once this stock is consumed, the affair is ended. Resources are seen as static and fixed tangible substances. This limited concept of resources has perplexed economists in the past and now it has crept into correction literature to create confusion there. Let us examine a more useful concept of resources that will help in assessing the nature and function of the sub rosa economy.

Economic resources are the result of the interaction between men and "neutral stuff."[7] For instance, uranium has existed for countless eons, but was not a resource until man developed uses for it. If a man functions at the animal level, he is buffeted about helplessly in a world of static and fixed quantities of resources. In certain parts of the world, tribes of men depend solely on the bounty of their environment for their livelihood. They move through the jungle until they reach a garden spot where bananas are available for them to eat. They consume the static supply of food and then move to a new garden spot—not unlike the grazing herds of primates moving through the jungles of Africa. For them, the Sykes statement noted above would be appropriate. It is less appropriate when one considers that resources include the inner qualities of man as well as the objects that surround him in his environment.

Man's reasoning ability is itself a resource in the broad sense of the word. Dictionary definitions show that "resources" are means to attain given ends, or that upon which one relies for aid. When man applies his intelligence in the use of the things he finds in his environment, he is able to make them useful for his own purposes. The example of the wandering tribe subsisting on bananas is an oddity in our contemporary world. Almost all peoples make better use of their environment. Relatively few are fortunate enough to live in moderate climates where food can be plucked from trees throughout the year; most people must apply their intelligence in order to survive in harsher climates where food and shelter are more difficult to attain.

Most of economic history is composed of descriptions of how man created resources where none existed before. A priori reasoning tells us that electricity existed as a force in the world even before man emerged from the primordial ooze, yet man roamed the earth for scores of centuries before he learned to harness electricity for his own use—to convert this "neutral stuff" into a resource. His array of tools did not include electricity even though he was surrounded by it and dimly aware of it. Eventually, the accumulated knowledge of his kind reached a state where he was able to make use of it, and thereby add a new resource to his stock of resources.

The same principles apply to the miniature societies of prisons. Inmates have access to quantities of "neutral stuff" of various kinds. Waste products are one example. These appear to be of no conceivable use to anyone and seem to be completely harmless as well. Appearing to be harmless and worthless, these wastes are not carefully controlled. Potato peelings may seem to be only garbage to the custodians, but they may be prized by inmates as a prime ingredient for a batch of homemade beer. Once the beer is produced, it clearly is a commodity that did not previously exist. Production of beer and alcoholic drinks is common in prison.

Using the expanded concept of resources as a *flow* instead of the limited concept of resources as a *stock,* it is not difficult to visualize some of the many possibilities for inmates to increase their stock of goods by applying their ability and intelligence to the problem of overcoming the scarcity of their world. One of the most unusual examples of this type of activity was discovered by Tom Murton during his brief career as a reform penologist at Tucker Prison Farm in Arkansas. He was astonished to see two inmates driving around the farm in a motor vehicle which they had fashioned from a frame, a steering mechanism, and different size tires and wheels—all driven by a Wisconsin engine connected via a chain drive. The inmates had constructed the amazing vehicle from waste scraps and pieces found around the farm.[8]

The vehicle example is perhaps extreme, but it illustrates a basic principle that must be understood if one hopes to comprehend the nature of the sub rosa system. The prison society contains a virtually unlimited supply of resources because a meaningful definition of resources must include the intelligence and ingenuity of men. Tangible materials are used in manufacturing processes carried out under enormously difficult conditions. End-less variations of services arise and flourish in response to identifiable demand situations.

SUBSISTENCE AND BEYOND

As with all economic systems, the illicit economy of male prisons furnishes answers to several basic questions: the fundamental problems evolve around *what* will be produced with the available resources, *how* the production will be accomplished, and *who* will get the goods and services produced. It is the way in which these questions are answerd that differs among economic systems. An economic system can be of the command type, in which case the basic questions are answered by government (central authority). In a tradition type of economy, economic activity has been carried on in certain ways for as long as anyone can remember, so custom provides the answers to the eco-nomic questions. In a market type of economy the basic questions are answered by impersonal forces: the interaction of the production sector and the consumption sector of the economy. Of course these two sectors are conceptualizations only and do not involve separate and distinct groups of people; one person or economic unit will be both a producer and a consumer. The market type of economy is unquestionably the most fascinating to study, and is the most complex of all systems. The sub rosa economy is most nearly a market economy.

When one considers the special nature of the sub rosa system, it is immediately obvious that the system does not primarily function to fulfill the same basic needs that other economic systems fulfill. Survival is still the basic goal of economic systems of most of the nations of the world, despite the talk of affluent societies. An economic system functions to provide the basic necessities, such as enough food to prevent starvation and enough shelter and clothing to avoid death by exposure to the elements.[9] In some developing countries, meeting these subsistence level needs uses up the available resources; in more industrialized nations, a surplus above the subsistence level is possible and more sophisticated needs are met as they arise.

Thus in one sense convicts live in a utopian world in which the basic subsistence is forthcoming without effort or uncertainty. Starvation or overexposure to the elements is not a threat in the inmate culture. Food comes to the individual at regular intervals in a ready-to-eat form, and ready-to-wear clothing is provided as the need arises. Shelter from the ele-ments is received by the individual as a matter of course. This subsistence level of living comes to the inmate without any effort on his part. The inmate may be required to work, but his work is almost totally unrelated to his economic well-being. Whether or not the inmate is required to work depends not upon his need, but upon the corrections theory in vogue at the time.[10]

While he may be punished for not working, he will not be denied the necessities of life.

Howard B. Gill points out that during the period of American penological history from about 1825 until 1925, nonproductive punitive labor was commonly used as a part of the prison program. Such activity stemmed from the prevailing view of the era that prisons were established to punish the incarcerated during their confinement as a part of the process of breaking his spirit. Nonproductive labor assignments consisted of tasks such as the carrying of a cannon shot from one end of the prison yard to the other or walking on a treadmill.[11] Our penitentiaries still emphasize work as a part of their program and it is not always clear whether work is considered to be therapy or punishment.

The economic activity of the incarcerated offender is severed from the motivating force of necessity that impels citizens of the outside world. Nor is there any association between quality and hours of work, for an inmate is not economically rewarded when he excels on the job. However, these generalizations apply only when one considers the formal economic system of the prison. Pondering the nature of the inmate's illegal economic activity returns the economist to more familiar terrain. While sub rosa economic activity need not be carried out to obtain the bare necessities, it can provide desired goods not otherwise available and can provide extra goods that normally are available in amounts too limited to satisfy the craving for such items. Thus the illegal system is concerned with provision of wants and needs of a more sophisticated and complex nature, which tend to be tied to psychological and sociological needs. However, in some cases they are physical in the sense that they are related to release of sexual tensions.

In order to achieve status and to establish ego-building uniqueness, inmates must operate within their own informal social system, since the formal system of the prison systematically denies them status and uniqueness. Our prison system impoverishes the offenders in a deliberate and methodical way. Gill lists the multiple elements of enforced prison poverty as (1) *deprivation* of everything other than bare necessities; (2) *monotony* in diet and daily routine; (3) *degradation* and loss of identity—partially due to (4) *uniformity* of treatment of prisoners; (5) *subservience* to rules; (6) lack of *recreation* opportunities; and (7) lack of *responsibility* even in minor decisions of daily existence; and (8) rules preventing fraternization with the guards, who represent the outside society.[12] Although definitions of poverty are necessarily relative to some arbitrary standard, most people in the American society would feel poor when subjected to the methodical deprivation described by Gill.

TRUNCATED SUPPLY AND INFERIOR GOODS

One finds that the sub rosa inmate economy exists within a special type of environment. On the one hand, uncertainty is eliminated in that a steady stream of necessities is forthcoming without any effort on the part of individuals within the group. On the other hand, the quantity and quality of the "manna from heaven" received leaves the recipients dissatisfied and the complete lack of some items disturbs them further. Their economy has scarcity imposed upon it by the keepers; whereas the outside economy has primarily the impersonal nature of the system to impose scarcity. Scarcity directly imposed by men upon other men allows the source of deprivation to be identified and hated. And more than this, the artificial scarcity created makes ordinarily insignificant transactions significant and grotesque transactions common.

One finds that the economic status of the prison community is unique in that the free society has deliberately designated the prison community as an island of poverty in the midst of a society of relative abundance. The supply of goods has been truncated or artificially cut off. Truncated supply results in prison demand for goods and services that would seem inconsequential or even bizarre to the free world denizen. Goods and services that would not be consumed at all outside the prison can attain exaggerated importance inside the prison simply because the inmates are denied the use of things that constitute a normal part of their living standard on the outside.

For example, the offender who engages in some relaxation and escapism on the outside by becoming pleasantly intoxicated on aged bourbon may be horrified and disgusted at the thought of getting drunk by sniffing glue. Once inside the prison walls, however, he not only finds that there is no bourbon available, but that there is no intoxicating substance even remotely like bourbon in quality. He finds that glue sniffing, though unpleasant initially, produces a reaction a little like the end result of drinking bourbon. He also quickly finds he is subject to considerable stress and needs a temporary escape from the harsh realities of prison life. If he further finds that glue is available through the sub rosa system, he may change his former opinion of glue sniffing and become a consumer. One might say that his tastes have changed because of the change in his circumstances. Although he may not be overly fond of glue, he has a demand for it simply because no better substitute for bourbon is at hand.

The glue sniffing example illustrates what economists call an *inferior good:* a product that is used only because higher quality items are not available or are too expensive. If and when a better quality product becomes available, demand for the inferior good decreases. When the inmate is released, his demand for glue for sniffing will disappear. In economic analysis, inferior goods are associated with levels of income. The very poor may consume a cheap type of food, not because better food is unavailable, because they cannot afford anything better. When they become more prosperous, they switch to a better grade of food. The prison situation differs in that many goods and services are denied the inmate even if he could afford them, as some affluent prisoners obviously could.

The fact that many types of goods and services as well as certain social and psychological satisfactions are forbidden to the convict accounts for some of the more bizarre aspects of the sub rosa economic system. Acts which are insignificant in the free society assume importance within the penitentiary. If a free world citizen pays a laundry worker to place an extra crease in his shirt, it is an act hardly worthy of note, as it is assumed to be a small matter of personal preference. When the convict pays a laundry worker to place a crease in his shirt it is significant, for he may be demonstrating to the convict world his power and economic acumen. He is expressing a modest version of the Veblenian "conspicuous consumption." In the free world, the inmate would attempt to excel in the standard American way of acquiring material goods coveted by others, especially material goods easily displayed to strangers as well as to friends. On the streets the inmate might drive the flashiest automobile on the block and wear dapper clothes. In prison, since he is required to be uniformly drab and poverty stricken, small adjustments to his uniform is his way of displaying success to friends and strangers alike—his mode of conspicuous consumption. Small uniform adjustments, a crease here and a tuck there, are no less significant on the inside than big automobiles on the outside.

EXTENT OF ILLICIT ACTIVITY

In *The Society of Captives* Sykes presents a roster of one day's disciplinary charges and the disposition of the charges.[13] Disciplinary charges are written complaints made to prison officials by guards who observe inmates violating rules. Table 3-1 reproduces that roster in order to indicate a substantial part of the violations involve economic activity or, to be more specific, a disruption in the flow of economic activity in the sub rosa system. Although Sykes did not present the roster for this purpose, even a cursory glance at Table 3-1 shows that much of the rule breaking within the institution consists of economic activity. The roles of producer and consumer are also evident; some of the charges involve production processes, some distribution activity, and others consumption.

The activities noted in Table 3-1 are the surface manifestations of a large amount of underground economic activity. This can be deduced by recalling the relationships among the activities of manufacturing, distribution, and consumption. In order to be a consumer in an economic system, a person must produce his own products, have current income, or draw upon a stock of accumulated wealth. For the prison economic system, one can rule out the possibility of entering the system with accumulated wealth to spend. The inmate may produce some items for his own use, but if he desires to purchase, barter, and trade in the system, he must become a producer of a good or a service in order to have income or trade goods. There are two sides to every transaction: there always must be a buyer and a seller, inasmuch as an

Table 3-1. Disciplinary Charges and Disposition

Charge		*Disposition*	
1.	Insolence and swearing while being interrogated	1.	Continue in segregation
2.	Threatening an inmate	2.	Drop from job
3.	Attempting to smuggle roll of tape into institution	3.	1 day in segregation with restricted diet
4.	Possession of contraband	4.	30 days' loss of privileges
5.	Possession of pair of dice	5.	20 days in segregation with restricted diet
6.	Insolence	6.	Reprimand
7.	Out of place	7.	Drop from job. Refer to classification committee for reclassification
8.	Possession of homemade knife, metal, and emery paper	8.	5 days in segregation with restricted diet
9.	Suspicion of gambling or receiving bets	9.	Drop from job and change Wing assignment
10.	Out of place	10.	15 days' loss of privileges
11.	Possession of contraband	11.	Reprimand
12.	Creating disturbance in Wing	12.	Continue in segregation
13.	Swearing at an officer	13.	Reprimand
14.	Out of place	14.	15 days' loss of privileges
15.	Out of place	15.	15 days' loss of privileges

expenditure for one person becomes income for the other party to the transaction.

In a primitive economy, consumer units may be self-sufficient by producing all the goods and services consumed or they may trade goods with each other. A more advanced economy has extensive specialization; that is, the producer achieves greater efficiency by concentrating his efforts upon the production of only one type of good or service. He then has a surplus of the specialty item and a scarcity of other desired items, which necessitates trade. A monetary system is a social innovation that makes this barter process operate much more smoothly and saves time and effort.

The economic activity in the inmate society is conducted on several levels. Inmates make goods for their own use, they trade and barter with other inmates, and there is also a distinct element of specialization and the use of a money substitute. These latter characteristics—specialization and money use,—make their economy a rather advanced and intricate system. A complex system requires extensive cooperation among the participants.

Without cooperation the cycle of economic activity would break down, for there must be a motivational system of some type to induce cooperation. In a market society the motivational system can be described in terms of profit motive, self-interest, or avarice—a participant has only his personal interest in mind as he takes part in economic activity by contributing to the productive processes and consuming a part of the fruit of the activity.

One might posit that inmates are not the most cooperative of people. After all, they are inmates, sequestered within prison walls, precisely because they could not cooperate adequately with the individuals of their community or obey their rules. In many cases, their lack of cooperation was manifested in their refusal to abide by the economic rules created by the free society. They attempted to gain income by means that were forbidden. They practice theft, robbery, fraud, burglary, or some other nonproductive activity, that results in the transfer of wealth without the creation of production or value. Society could not, or would not, tolerate this type of nonproductive activity inasmuch as it destroys the operation of the economy.

In order for the sub rosa economy to operate effectively, it too must have a means of securing and insuring the cooperation of the individuals involved. Even though self-interest is present as a motivational influence in the sub rosa system, this does not assure cooperation in its fullest sense nor does it prevent the transfer of wealth by nonproductive predatory activity. Self-interest can trigger economic activity that is productive, but it can also trigger nonproductive or predatory activity. Ground rules or laws are needed to channel self-interest into productivity so that individuals are motivated to produce (create) goods and services rather than to steal them. Ironically, the inmate culture also finds it necessary to formulate and enforce laws relating to economic activity. The system cannot tolerate too great a degree of predatory accumulation of wealth unless the predatory activities are aimed at the prison staff, who are outside the system. The sub rosa system must have productive activity, just as the free world economy.

The inmate code is the legal environment of the sub rosa system. The code approves any kind of abuse against the prison administrators, who represent the society that rejected and imprisoned them; conversely, the code does not tolerate abuses of one member of the culture by another member. If the inmate violates the code in some minor way, he is socially isolated. If his offense is grave, he is beaten or killed by the inmates. Thus, his society in microcosm controls him in exactly the same fashion that the outside society control its members. Fear of retribution by fellow inmates forces the inmate to cooperate. Of course, a few strong believers in the inmate code are "moral" in relation to the beliefs of the culture and have internal restraints or moral scruples against violating the tenets of the code. Beyond these internal restraints, nonetheless, there is always the threat of coercion.

If the inmate cannot adapt to prison life and learn to function within the inmate social system, he eventually reaches the end of the road as a human being. He is placed in a prison within a prison, which is known as the incorrigible unit. In this place for the extremely alienated, the inmate becomes little more than a vegetable, for his life consists of a cell, a few meals a day, pacing, and sleeping.[14]

GOODS AND SERVICES IN THE SYSTEM

While the market economy of the prison has both goods and services, it is heavily oriented toward services. This tendency is understandable when one considers that the provision of services does not create the storage problems, with their attendent risk of discovery, created by the manufacture and distribution of goods. Commodities present a special problem because they must be hidden and secretly transported. Stores that are discovered are confiscated by prison guards, causing business losses and recessions in the system.

Prison regulations specify the merchandise that may be circulated within a prison population and anything not specified is contraband. Many items circulated within the inmate economic system are not contraband per se. For example, candy, tobacco, and toilet articles can be obtained legally at the prison canteen, which is part of the prison's formal economy. Although these articles are legally obtained, they may become a part of illegal traffic later. When sold at the prison canteen, they are meant for the personal consumption of the purchaser. The most common case of legally obtained goods being converted to illicit use is the purchase of cigarettes at the canteen. The legally obtained cartons and packs of cigarettes become money for the illicit transactions of the system. Other legally obtained goods become intermediate goods in the trade channels of the sub rosa system. The illicit economic system, to some extent, feeds upon the officially sanctioned economic system. In turn, value is created in the sub rosa system to enhance the individual's standard of living. Since the canteen selection is limited and the inmate is allowed to purchase only a limited amount of a small selection of merchandise, only the sub rosa system can bring abundance.

MONEY

As a common custody practice, maximum and medium security prisons in the United States do not allow their prison populations to use the currency, coins, and demand deposits of commercial banks, which make up the official money supply of the United States. Inmates must use book credits, a variation of the demand deposit, for the purchase of consumer items at the prison commissary. If relatives or friends mail money to the inmate, the prison mail censors remove the money and have it deposited to the inmate's account. Visitors are watched carefully so they cannot pass money or other contraband to the inmate. A few prisons allow coins of small denomination to circulate legally within the prison and some sanction the use of tokens as substitutes for coins.

These fairly rigorous controls do not prevent the illegal circulation of currency and coin within the inmate population. They do, however, change the nature of the usefulness of currency and coin. Currency becomes a contraband commodity within the system instead of a means of facilitating transactions. Currency becomes one of the long list of smuggled items which can be secretly purchased in the sub rosa system. As a commodity, currency may be needed for escape or for paying off a corrupt guard, but it is not needed or commonly used as the medium of exchange for illicit transactions.

The sub rosa economy depends upon an entirely different form of money for its illicit transactions: cigarettes constitute the illicit medium of exchange. The literature of correction indicates the acceptance of cigarettes as money throughout the correctional system. There appear to be considerable advantages to the use of "cigarette money": cigarettes are not contraband items and are not subject to seizure by guards, nor can the inmate be punished for being found with them in his possession. Trade is facilitated because of the rather stable, well known standard of value; all brands of cigarettes within the prison have the same monetary value per package or carton and this monetary value is known to everyone.

Replacing worn-out money is not a problem to the inmate culture as it is in the free world. Cigarettes serve a dual purpose since they have intrinsic value as a commodity in addition to their value as a medium of exchange. The medium of exchange does not wear out because inmate smokers are constantly consuming (smoking) the cigarettes, and replacing them legally (buying them) through the formal economic system of the prison. To make an analogy with the outside society, it is as if foreign ambassadors were continually collecting worn-out bills and coins and replacing them with new ones for United States citizens, thus sparing the United States the trouble and expense of performing this service for itself.

An additional advantage of cigarette money is that it conveniently comes in three denominations. Very minor illicit purchases can be made with individual cigarettes, slightly larger purchases can be made with packages of twenty cigarettes, and large transactions can be handled with cartons of ten packages. Thus cigarettes have most of the characteristics of a substance considered suitable for money: a widely accepted standard of value, durability (at least in the sense that replacement is no problem), and divisibility.

Since the sub rosa system has an adequate medium of exchange, the specialization and division of labor which is characteristic of advanced, complex economic systems becomes possible. The presence of money in a system facilitates trade, allows the extension of credit, and makes possible the accumulation of purchasing power. Money opens the door for the operation of a sophisticated economic system.

SELF-PRODUCERS AND RECIPROCAL TRADE

Far from taking place in a vacuum, sub rosa economic activity is part of the total interaction taking place in the inmate culture—a culture where the upholding of group values and solidarity is a central theme.[15] As early as 1936 Ellis Ash, after spending four months in the State Reformatory at Monroe, Washington, as a participant observer, concluded that "conniving" was a "basic process in the interaction between prisoners."[16] Prisoners create products, goods and services for one another. And sometimes they simply reallocate those goods provided by the prison officials because the inmate code demands that products be shared.[17] Thus, a part of the economic activity is of a casual nature—not profit oriented, but rather an expression of group unity. Goods are shared in a balanced reciprocity within small cliques as befitting the ideal expressed in the inmate code. This particular type of activity helps to pass the time as well as helping to express solidarity. Conniving breaks the monotony.

Just as inmate cliques share, men who live in the close proximity of a cell frequently divide economic goods to solidify their social relationships. The story of two convicts carefully making out their commissary lists, told by David Lamson, vividly portrays the manner in which two cellmates shared their goods. The story also demonstrates some of the pathos of being condemned men.[18]

> "You going to order oranges again? Then I'll put cheese on my list. Now, what about candy?"
> "How about those Toddle bars?"
> "The dam nuts get in my teeth. Wonder what these Tango bars are like?"
> "What kind was it you brought in here from the other cell? They were swell."
> "They aren't on the list this month."
> "Well, let's get another two dozen milk chocolate, and we can use them to make chocolate out of, instead of ordering cocoa. And I'll order a box of salted pecans, and we can wash the salt off and bake 'em and stir up a mess of candy with the milk chocolate and plain sugar, and that will make the chocolate go twice as far."

The conversation soon shifts to bedding.

> "You been beefing about the way the wool blankets scratch; you going to order cotton?"

"Why not sheets?"

"They'd get too dirty. The laundry don't like to do them oftener than once a month."

"Yeah, but if I did order 'em I'd only have 'em about a month before I go up."

The inmate conversation at this juncture is clearly illustrating the economic concept of economizing—the heart of decision making in economics. "Economizing" means the allocation of limited resources among alternative ends in a way that will maximize one's satisfaction. The discussion continues:

"Yeah, but I'm going to wait and see, now I've waited this long. God, I wish I'd ordered 'em when I first came up, like you did. Anyway, maybe you'll go out and I'll inherit yours."

"Yeah. You wait for me to go out, you'll scratch for a long time. Go on and get some; I'm tired of watching you mess around with those silly bath-towels, trying to use them for sheets."

"No, sir, I won't do it. I'm not going to blow my money for blankets until I'm sure I'm going to get some good out of 'em The man sure won't let me take 'em to the Birdcage with me if I do go up!"[19]

Coffee and Food

"We'll get it one way or another." A convict, who later was killed by the police after an attempted escape, told of fashioning a hollow tube, one inch in diameter, which he inserted into a burlap sack containing one hundred pounds of regular prison coffee. By agitating the sack, he was able to siphon out a pound or so at a time. Although this man had been a semi-trusty and clerk, who could gain access to the supply room, almost all inmates have opportunities to pilfer prison supplies.[20]

The oppressing monotony of prison life is partially broken by the simple and familiar events involved in food preparation. Coffee or food is methodically stolen from the kitchen or dining room. In the cell, cooking utensils must be organized, the coffee boiled and the food prepared and consumed, perhaps in cooperation with the men in an adjoining cell. Probably as much planning and preparation goes into a simple evening coffee hour in cell block 41 as is involved in the local Junior Chamber of Commerce annual awards banquet. Men devise elaborate electric cookers and numerous mechanical gadgets for heating coffee in their cells. Steam radiators can boil water and cook choice items. Inmates may even collect oily rags to use as fuel for boiling water.[21] During these activities, inmates must keep a lookout for patrolling guards. A small mirror held outside of the cell bars allows the inmate to see an approaching officer. This, of course, adds an air of excitment and pleasure to the occasion.

Certain types of food take on an exaggerated importance in prison because the prisoners do not receive them as often as they desire in standard prison fare. A "sweet tooth" must be satisfied largely from the prisoner's own meager resources—by legal purchase in the commissary or by illicit means. During the 1972 riot at the Attica, New York, State Prison, an incident occured that pathetically demonstrates this point. During the early states of the riot, several correctional officers were retaking a portion of the prison which had fallen to the prisoners. The following incident occurred as they entered C Block:

> There they encountered a young obese inmate clad in a football helmet and carrying a baseball bat and a pail. When the uprising began, he had eagerly joined in looting the officer's mess, filling a pail full of sweets and other foods never available to inmates. He had retired to his cell to eat, while the rebellion moved on to D yard. Now he was returning to the officers' mess for more when he was apprehended and subdued by the advancing officers.[22]

The obsession of the Attica inmate with the pail is understandable if one considers the fare furnished in the formal system. The following example is an account of a new inmate at Joliet Prison in Illinois being introduced to the prison diet and discussing it with his more experienced cellmate:

> Bill walked back to his bunk and sat down. He began to eat.
> "What's that stuff in the beans?" I asked. "That stuff with the hairs sticking out of it?"
> "Fatback," Bill said. "Fatback is for protein, man. They got to give you some protein. Whatsamatter, don't you like hogfat?"
> I shook my head.
> "Well, I'll eat it," he announced.
> I handed him the bowl. "Eat it all. I'm not hungry."
> "I had a hard time gettin' used to it at first," he said.
> "How often do you get that stuff?"
> "Oh, you get fatback in all your beans and all your greens and in most all vegetables. They cook about everything in hog fat. Boil it, fry it, you know."
> I was silent.
> "Couple times a week they give you a meatball. Sometimes they call it hamburger, sometimes sails-bary steak. 'Bout the size of a silver dollar and mixed with filler like bread or crackers. Tough as golf balls."[23]

Prostitution

Male homosexual prostitution is a significant activity in the services category. However, male prisons are not seething beds of passion and sexual activity. Although estimates vary, it is thought that from 30 to 40 percent of all male inmates have homosexual contacts while incarcerated.[24] Differences in estimates of the extent of homosexual activities depend upon several factors in the prison setting being studied: degree of prison security, backgound of inmates, and length of prison sentence.[25] Most inmates who have homosexual relations in prison consider themselves to be heterosexual, and, for the most part, the inmates who abstain from homosexual relations take a philosophical view toward the activity around them.

Homosexual activity occurs for several reasons other than the release of physical tension. Maintaining that the men are seeking emotional relationships that are meaningful to serve as substitutes for normal relationships with women on the outside, John H. Gagnon and William Simon[26] point out that this behavior is similar to that of all male communities under extreme stress. Another motivation is to validate one's masculinity and to stand as "a symbol of resistance to the prison environment. [27] Peter C. Buffum[28] explains that the man whose masculine validation was his sexual prowess finds himself without this verification in prison; thus, he continues to play an aggressive masculine role with male inmates as his prey. Men who are in prison do not represent a cross section of American males coming from all strata of society; rather they are mostly deprived men from the deprived segments of society. For these men sexual experiences are concrete. Involving little fantasy, their experiences reinforce their masculinity and serve as conversation material when feats of triumph are discussed with other men.[29]

The inmates who play the agressive roles of "jockers" or "wolves" generally have little homosexual experience outside the prison. Their prison relationships more often than not are fleeting. Charles R. Tittle, in studying homosexuality in male prisons, interviewed one inmate who indicated that he visited one of the prison prostitutes once a week and paid five or six packages of cigarettes for sexual relief. The inmate emphasized that he sought only physical relief and rarely, if ever, felt any affection for his partner. Tittle believes that this inmate's attitude is typical of such relationships.[30]

In cases where the relationship is more of the nature of a temporary marriage, a stereotyped courtship takes place. Seduction usually follows a set pattern: the prison-wise con befriends a new inmate, shows him around, and teaches him the rules of the game. The old con will probably try to impress him with the idea that many wolves and punks are good friends with the implication that the two of them can be too. The wolves will shower presents on new inmates and do favors for them until they can develop a recognized, somewhat stable relationship.

Prison argot distinguishes between inmates who allow themselves to be forced into a female role (punks) and those inmates who prefer the female role (queens or fags). Almost all new prisoners go through a testing period during which they are in danger of becoming punks. A friend of ours who has served more than twenty years in a number of different prisons, told us of the straightforward way in which such testing is often conducted and the way that he handled it. Upon being locked in a prison dormitory where he was not known, he was almost immediately surrounded by a group of inmates. One of the larger inmates stood in front of him and stated his simple proposition: "fuck or fight." The proper response for the untested inmate was to immediately strike the propositioning con, thereby starting a fight. This spontaneous response assured him that he would not be considered to be sexual fodder for all the wolves in the dormitory. He did not intend to be chaste, just selective.

At times, the testing period can be more of an ordeal and involve more violence than a simple fist fight. An inmate in California's Soledad Prison describes his decision to seek help from the guards after he was approached by members of a gang which had recently raped and killed a prisoner. Some time later, two of the gang members approached him and informed him that he was next to be killed if he did not become a homosexual. The inmate's alternatives were: (1) to become a punk, (2) to get a weapon and fight; or, (3) become an informer. He chose the latter after a brief period of thought.[31]

Inmates playing the aggressive sexual role will frequently avoid such outright violence in their attempts to transform a new inmate into a punk by using the coercion of debt. Once a new inmate gets into debt to a wolf, he may find that he has no way to pay other than to become a prostitute. This process is illustrated by Piri Thomas as he advises a friend who has recently been sent to prison and tries to extricate him from a bad situation.

> "Tico, we're more than cousins, kid, we're brothers. Just handle yourself right, don't make fast friends, and act cool. Don't play and joke too much, and baby, don't, just don't, accept candy or smokes from stranger cons. You might end up paying for it with your ass."
>
> He kept on looking at the concrete walk and his face grew red and the corners of his mouth got a little too white. "Piri, I've been hit on already," he said.
>
> I thought, *My God, he's got a jailhouse gorilla reception already.* "Yeah," I prompted, "and. . ."
>
> "Well, I got friendly with this guy named Rube."
>
> Rube was a muscle bound degenerate whose sole ambition in life was to cop young kids' behinds. "Yeah," I said, "and so. . ."
>
> "Well, this cat has come through with smokes and food and candy and, well, he's a spic like me and he talked about the street outside and about guys we know outside and he helped me out with favors, you know real friendly.". . .
>
> *My God*, I thought, *what can I tell him?* Tico had to show man or he was finished. Rube would use that first time to hold him by

threatening to tell everybody that he screwed him. And if any-
body found out, every wolf in the joint would want to cop. The
hacks would hear about it and they would put Tico on A-1 tier
where all the faggots were, and he'd be a jailhouse punk. "What
do you owe him, Tico?" I asked.

"About three cartons of smokes, fourteen candy bars, some
canned food, and a couple of undershirts."[32]

While the punk is forced into his predicament either by direct or
indirect application of force, his role does have economic overtones. The punk
is a reluctant prostitute—an unwilling provider of a service in the sub rosa
economy of the inmate culture. The punk may be courted with gifts and, in
some cases, he may continue to receive presents and favors from several
inmates after being attached to one wolf. Whether or not his economic
benefits continue depends largely upon his ability to become the "property"
of a wolf who will provide protection from other wolves in addition to
providing some of the amenities of life. The role of the prison punk and the
trouble that it can cause are depicted by Lester Douglas Johnson as he
describes an incident occurring in a Kansas prison where he was serving
time.[33]

There was a boy we will call Billy who worked in the power
plant. He was a nice-looking boy, rather effeminate, with blue eyes
and blond hair. He was not a genuine homosexual. He was one of
those who had decided to take the line of least resistance. He was
"married" to a big, brutal, sadistic pervert who enjoyed the
popularity of being "daddy." He was very jealous and had been
involved in serveral serious scrapes because of Billy's delight in
trifling. Billy knew this man would fight for him, and this was
pleasing to him. He would flirt with other men in the hopes that
there would be trouble.

A new man came to work at the power plant, and Billy, true to
form, made his play. The fellow was con-wise and ignored him.
This infuriated the boy, and he decided to get the man into a jam.
He went and told his jocker that the fellow had propositioned
him. This lead to words, then real action. In the fight that ensued,
Billy's boy friend was getting the worst of it. He drew a shiv and
began cutting the unarmed man. He stabbed him eighteen times,
and as he was doing the bloody job, Billy was sitting on a ledge
high above, shouting, "Kill him, Daddy! Kill him, Daddy!"

Johnson believes that these sexual entanglements cause more
trouble inside the prison than they do on the streets. Outside the prison, a
man can break up with his girl and walk away and forget it; while inside, the
inmate who loses a "girl" to another con feels the machismo pressure of the
inmate culture. He cannot give up the punk without retaliating for fear of
losing honor and prestige in the inmate culture.[34]

A punk may operate within the sub rosa economic system in a fashion simlar to the "B girl" or "golddigger" on the outside. To make this analogy, reviewing the economic behavior of these two types of women would be valuable. The B girl may be observed in bars and night spots where the primary clientele is male, preferable a lounge that offers a stimulating floor show with exotic dancers or "nudie" films. The B girl hustles the customers for drinks and receives a percentage of the take on the extra drinks sold. The drinks may be water that is colored to look like alcohol or an expensive bottle of wine that is never actually delivered to the table. The B girl is differentiated from the prostitute in that she does not intend to deliver her sexual favors, but rather, excites the male customer by trying to convince him that he is actually courting her and she is just on the verge of being seduced. The golddigger operates in much the same way except that she is an amateur without a base of operation and the backing of a formal business organization. Pretending affection and seeming always to be vitally interested in sexual intercourse, the golddigger gleans gifts, favors, and other economic benefits from her lover before leaving him unrequited and moving to another victim.

Prison punks sometimes assume these B girl or golddigger behavior patterns as a means of earning income in the sub rosa economy. Clemmer notes that prison "prostitutes" flirt with prison wolves in order to receive gifts of candy and tobacco, but attempt to avoid actual sexual contact if possible.[35]

Even though Clemmer refers to these social types as prostitutes in the above example, their behavior is more closely allied to the B girl and golddigger roles on the street. Since the outside society distinguishes between the roles of B girl, golddigger, and prostitute, these distinctions may be useful in assessing the inmate culture. On the outside, the prostitute contracts to actually deliver her sexual favors and she does deliver; it is a forthright business transaction with no overtones of fraud or chicanery. Both parties gain satisfaction, albeit a different type, from the arrangement and there is usually no victim who might desire retribution.

The prison community does have its share of outright and forthright prostitutes in the more limited sense of the term and the job functions associated with it. Mike Misenheimer illustrates the straightforwardness of the prostitution transaction as follows:[36]

> One morning a friend of mine standing in the messhall breakfast line felt a tug on his sleeve. He sleepily turned toward his accoster and was asked in a desperate whisper, "Man, I need two packs! You want some head?"
>
> The "punk" was, of course, offering to commit oral sodomy. It was 6 A.M.
>
> My friend grumpily declined. We watched the "punk" proposition several more cons before he finally found a customer. They

slipped out into the morning darkness of "Bean Alley," where the enterprising young salesman no doubt earned his two packs.

This incident is unusual only in regard to time and place. It is repeated many times with variations of time and place, characters, and price. Three "reelers" or two "Big D's" (pills) might be the price rather than coffee or cigarettes. More often than not, the customer will be the one to propose the transaction.

In the value system of the inmate culture, the homosexual activity of the wolves, punks, and casual couples is considered to be situational, or behavior that is a direct response to imprisonment. The inmate culture has strong machismo values which are most likely a carryover from the lower class socioeconomic background from which the majority of inmates came. In the free society, the machismo elements of the lower class value system stigmatize masturbation by adult males. The shame is not moralistic in origin since very young males, say thirteen or fourteen years old, are expected to masturbate—even encouraged to do so—due to their inexperience in the seduction of females. Yet the machismo values lead to the belittling and dishonoring of the adult male who is foolish enough to admit that he masturbates. Such a male is suspect because a "real man" would be able to release his sexual tensions in an "acceptable" seduction of a female. With the value system of this stratum of society, conquest of many females is admirable, but marriage is also acceptable because not everyone can be adept at seduction or because a man must "do the right thing" when one of his conquests becomes pregnant.

Males who are socialized in this machismo oriented system develop an intense sense of shame about masturbation. They may feel so strongly about it that they attempt never to relieve sexual tension except through intercourse with a woman or by a "wet dream." Being a sign of weakness not to be tolerated in oneself, men will go to great lengths to avoid masturbation. When their needs become pressing, they may suddenly decide to seduce a woman whom they ordinarily find loathesome. A standard joke around barrooms illustrates this decision. The somewhat inebriated male who is becoming frantic because the evening is wearing on and no desirable female partner can be located, focuses his attention upon an aging, overweight, slovenly female barfly that he would not speak to earlier in the evening. As he begins his desperate courtship, he turns to her and says, "I'm going to drink until you begin to look good." If his insulting remark penetrates her alcoholic haze and ruins his seduction scene, he perceives that there is only one alternate left open to him. He must, despite his limited funds, hurry off into the night to seek out a professional prostitute—preferably an attractive prostitute, but any prostitute if necessary.

The "morning-after" is filled with anxiety because of his fear of venereal disease and shortage of operating funds. Yet he knows that he has done the only "manly thing." It was merely "bad luck" that kept him from scoring with a young, desirable, and clean female. His friends will readily reinforce his attitudes by sympathizing with his "bad run of luck," but none would think of suggesting that masturbation might have been a preferable alternative to the unfortunate evening. Thus the machismo values place a strong taboo on masturbation based on "manliness" rather than on parental teachings or religious dogma. Sex is necessary to manhood, but masturbation is not sex: it is an unacceptable weakness.

The value system also places a strong taboo on homosexual activity; however, the frenzied male who is so hapless that he is unable to locate even a homely prostitute may allow himself to be approached by an overt male homosexual. His situation is considered to be so desperate that he may allow a male homosexual to perform fellatio upon him. Again, it will be permissible for him to tell his friends of this incident if he is particularly careful to emphasize that he made a thorough search and could locate no female whatever.

The machismo values stress aggressiveness and conquest. The intoxicated female barfly, the ugly prostitute, and the overt male homosexual are all objects of contempt. Still, in a preference scale, they are to be ranked above masturbation as acceptable sexual outlets. The male who must resort to masturbation is a miserable failure. Not only will he strive to keep his masturbation a secret from his friends, but he will also experience a deep sense of guilt and "lost manhood." Sexual prowess, in this machismo oriented lower class structure, is a necessity for conversation and prestige as well as for physical release. First, the male must convince his friends that he has a strong sex drive and second he must convince them that he is successful in satisfying his strong sex drive by making numerous conquests. Emotional involvement with a sexual partner is considered to be a by-product of a sustained relationship with a fiancee or a wife, but it is unnecessary for the sex act.

A rough ranking of "conquest prestige" attached to the sexual acts in the lower class machismo culture is presented in Table 3-2. Prestige can only come from the conquistador's peers. The right hand colum in Table 3-2 shows the conditions that must accompany the event for the appropriate recognition to be awarded by his friends. If the conditions are not met, the prestige bestowed may be reduced or even cancelled. Sexual activity is ranked from very high prestige, which entitles the participant to be a braggart, to deplored acts that must be shamefully kept a secret from everyone.

The lower class American male attitudes expressed in Table 3-2 represent an *ideal,* they do not describe actual behavior. For example, a man who may really have a strong preference for cunnilingus will most likely keep this a secret from his friends and is apt to feel that something is "wrong" with him. Or a man who has never seduced a virgin is prone to feel a sense of "loss" and may harbor resentment that his wife denied him this event by allowing herself to be seduced by someone else. The more conforming of the

Table 3-2. Sexual Conquest Prestige in Machismo—Oriented Culture

Very High Prestige

(Calls for frequent & discreet bragging)

Event	*Group Requirements*
1. Attractive young single girl is induced to perform fellatio	Girl must not be below age of consent
2. Attractive young married women in a higher social class is induced to perform fellatio	Social position of the woman must preclude her as a prospective wife for the ingroup
3. Attractive young single virgin is induced to perform coitus	(See Number 1)[1]
4. Attractive young nonvirgin is induced to perform coitus	(See Number 1)
5. Attractive young married woman in higher social class is induced to perform coitus	(See Number 2)

Medium Prestige

(Occasional discreet bragging appropriate)

6. Attractive young virgin is obtained as wife	Must have potential to unlease hidden passions
7. Attractive young nonvirgin is obtained for wife	Original seduction must have been a "mistake" long since lived down. Preferably the seducer will be unknown to the husband
8. Attractive young widow is obtained for wife	Must have been faithful to former husband
9. Attractive young divorcee is obtained for wife	Must have waged valiant fight to save a marriage destroyed by worthless ex-husband
10. Extraordinarily attractive young single girl allows seducer to perform cunnilingus on her	Seducer must establish that he could not get her to perform coitus and could not have made the conquest otherwise. Must not express a preference for cunnilingus[2]

Table 3-2. (Continued)

Adequate Prestige

(Smirking appropriate once group is informed indirectly)

11. Plain, but likable, young single girl induced to perform fellatio — Not *too* young

12. Plain, but likable, young single girl induced to perform coitus — (See Number 11)

13. Plain, but extraordinarily passionate, wife is obtained — Husband must be able to "keep up" with demands made on him. Wife must be faithful[3]

14. Plain, but sexually adequate, wife is obtained — Must have other qualities, preferably a good cook and housekeeper

Tolerated

(Group will commiserate with male member)

15. Undesirable female barfly type induced to perform fellatio — Must have made a thorough search for a more suitable partner

16. Undesirable female barfly type induced to perform coitus — (See Number 15)

17. Wife of another member in same social class is seduced — Husband must be unpopular with ingroup or unknown to them

18. Attractive young prostitute is paid to perform fellatio — Must have made every effort to get sex without "paying for it"

19. Attractive prostitute is paid to perform coitus — Coitus is "cheaper" than fellatio

20. Unattractive prostitute is paid to perform fellatio — Ugly prostitutes are cheaper than attractive prostitutes

21. Unattractive prostitute is paid to perform coitus — Cheaper yet

22. Being masturbated by any prostitute — Being masturbated by a female is more acceptable than self-stimulation[4]

Table 3-2. (Continued)

23.	Subject is picked up by male homosexual who performs fellatio on him without charging a fee	All possible means of obtaining a female must have been exhausted. Must be infrequent occurrence
24.	Anal intercourse performed on male homosexual—no fee	(See Number 23)

Negative Status

(Act must be kept secret to avoid stigma)

25.	Masturbation	Acceptable for inexperienced males in early teens or preteens
26.	Preference for performing cunnilingus on women	(See Number 10)[5]
27.	Another male performing anal intercourse on subject	Must be kept secret at all costs
28.	Performing fellatio on another male	(See Number 27)

---

[1] The perception of an appropriate age may be faulty among the dim-witted. We once arrested an adult male for the rape of his two year old step-daughter. Not realizing that the inmate culture detests child rapers, he was heard to brag to jail companions, "I got me a virgin."

[2] An act of cunnilingus performed upon someone else's wife, whatever her social status, would be unacceptable. The group would tend to view the seducer as a "homosexual by proxy" because the woman's vagina could be presumed to have recently contained her husband's penis.

[3] The wife may seem extraordinarily passionate only because the husband is so inept that she rarely achieves the fulfillment of an orgasm. Male members of this lower socio-economic class appear to place no premium upon a female orgasm, nor to give it any place in their discussion other than a sort of curiosity. It is unlikely that the husband or his peers will perceive of this as a problem. If the wife complains or leaves the husband, they will express bafflement. In fact, this bewilderment is expressed in many of the country music songs so popular with the group; a large number of the songs have the theme of a male being deeply saddened because of a straying wife or girl friend who, without apparent reason, looks elsewhere for tenderness. Convicts and other male groups frequently talk about the "gang-shag" where in a single or married female has intercourse with several men within a short period of time. While the reason for female participation in the gang-shag has complex psychological and sociological nuances, one contributing factor is probably the lack of concern about the female orgasm in the values of the participating males. Aroused, but unfulfilled by intercourse with the first male, the female participant subsequently agrees to have intercourse with additional males. Admittedly, more complex theories are required to explain this behavior, still the physiological factor should not be overlooked altogether.

Table 3-2. (Continued)

[4]Prostitutes whose modus operandi is masturbation of their customers fall into two categories. One category consists of highly attractive young women who want to make some money without plunging wholeheartedly into prostitution. These semi-prostitutes frequent expensive bars where their personal attractiveness makes it possible for them to command relatively high fees ($20 for example) to perform a service less desirable to their customer than coitus. Once they convince the customer that they will not engage in coitus, the service can be quickly performed in an automobile or a dark corner booth in a bar. The girl incurs no overhead for motel rooms or other expenses required by coitus. The second category of specialists comprises aging prostitutes who have trouble attracting customers because their beauty and suppleness has faded. They work in dark movie theaters where the customer cannot get a close look at them and charge a relatively low fee ($5).

[5]A preference for cunnilingus is considered to be "unmanly" because the woman is thought to be dominant during such an act, while the male is not making a true "conquest"—he is viewed as "accommodating" the woman and being temporarily under her control. *She* is making the conquest. Myths are commonly told about males who were enticed by lovely women to perform cunnilingus and whose lives were ruined because they "liked it." The group recognizes that a beautiful woman may tempt a man into "submission" occasionally. He can receive prestige for the act only if the woman is a highly elusive and a much sought after prize who cannot be obtained without considerable "concessions." A preference for cunnilingus causes a male group member to be stigmatized as "queer for women." The group discourages younger members from experimenting with cunnilingus by making statements which imply that available women are "unwashed" and that they "smell bad." Digital penetration of a woman's vagina is called "playing stinky finger." Comments are often made that "once you get past the smell, you've got it licked." This latter statement seems designed to recognize that the temptation exists, but it is to be resisted. The Machismo oriented culture has myths that attribute superhuman sensuality to acts of oral sex. The male who has received fellatio from an attractive woman is the object of envy among his peers who express belief that he has experienced delights beyond comprehension. Other myths attribute the same mystical delights to females who are recipients of cunnilingus. Tales are told of men who, being overtly "queer for women", lead astray faithful wives and lovers. Such men are feared as are lesbians. Within the lower class social structure, both the male members and the lesbians appear to widely believe the common myth that "once she has been seduced by a woman, she will never want a man." These myths have an impact on the group members. An old burglar who has served many terms in prison once told us of his family troubles. His wife had been committed to a mental hospital during his last prison term. He earnestly believed that she had been driven insane by a lover that she took during his prison term. The lover, whom he knew only by reputation, had driven her insane by constantly performing cunnilingus on her. He was convinced that the pleasures of cunnilingus were so intense that no woman could long maintain her sanity if she permitted herself to indulge. His attitude was not unusual.

group members, however, will internalize these attitudes as a part of their code of morality. A strictly conformist male will attempt to avoid the need to masturbate even if he is in a strange city far away from anyone who knows him. Perhaps such a man is away from his home and wife for just a few days. His physical needs for sex are not overwhelming nor is he lacking in emotional satisfaction and affection in his home life. Furthermore, he may feel no need to be unfaithful to his wife for the sake of obtaining variety in his sex life.

Still, this man may have internalized the machismo values to such an extent that he will forego masturbation and visit a prostitute during his brief time away from home.

Prison inmates are drawn largely from the machismo oriented lower class that we have been describing. Understanding the sex attitudes of that group helps one to understand sexual behavior in male prisons. The new prisoner finds that the inmate population has the same basic attitudes about sex as his friends outside of the prison. Thus, the new prisoner is faced with a dilemma; he knows that masturbation is taboo, but he also knows that homosexual activity is taboo. He must select the lesser of two evils if he is to satisfy his sexual drives. His personal preferences will, of course, play an important part in his selection. Yet an initial decision to avoid homosexual activity may be modified with the passage of time.

The convict's decision making in respect to his sexual preferences will be affected by the machismo beliefs that he already knows and which he also finds to exist in the prison. Certain types of male-to-male sex acts can occur without both parties being stigmatized as homosexuals. He can, for example, allow another male to perform fellatio on him or he can perform anal intercourse on another male. Both of these acts are of the aggressive conquest variety which are acceptable behavior outside of the prison as well as inside. In fact, such behavior is more admirable than masturbation. The prestigious inmate leader is not stigmatized for having a "boy", rather he is admired. The less prestigious wolf or jocker social type is lacking in status not because of his pursuit of boys, but rather for his crudeness and excessive application of force. As indicated in Table 3-2, both masturbation and homosexual contact are low status events, but certain carefully defined types of homosexual contacts rank higher than masturbation.

Ambivalent feelings surrounding the choice between the two are shown by inmates. The following shows, first of all, that the writer accepts an outside value system which makes masturbation shameful. This assumption is based on his own preinstitution socialization in the machismo culture, hence the "social stigma." The comment also carries the implication that no self-respecting man would masturbate on his own volition—the institution "forces" him to the dastardly deed.

> Behind prison walls, masturbation does not carry the same social stigma that it does outside. A con is often heard to proclaim, "Tonight is 'jack' night, baby!" It is said in a tone that both condemns the system that forces him to perform this act and praises "self" for using this outlet rather than one of the other more (to him) unnatural outlets.[37]

Most of the staff members in prison are there to perform the custody (guarding) function. State systems seldom pay their prison guards well. Being drawn from roughly the same socioeconomic class as the prisoners, the guards have largely the same value orientation toward sex. Guards are prone to look with a degree of tolerance and sympathy on the behavior of the wolves or jockers, but—like the inmates—they hold in contempt the activities of the punks and the queens or fags. The queens or "homosexuals by preference" are viewed as undesirables to be segregated within the prison as much as possible. James Blake, a prison queen (although he officially denied it), describes the situation that he found upon being committed to the Florida State Penitentiary at Raiford.[38]

> My cell was near the end of a long narrow corridor, and to reach
> it I passed Cell G-5, a notorious den I'd heard of in the county
> jail. Here the overt homosexuals lived in perfumed, screaming lurid
> celebrity, wearing earrings, their faces garishly painted. A line hung
> across the cell was draped mysteriously with feminine undergar-
> ments. I marveled at the official attitude, which seemed to be one
> of contemptuous tolerance.
>
> The strange did manage to roam at certain times, I later learned,
> and were able to rendezvous with the jailhouse lovers, who provided
> them with cigarettes, makeup and the things that make a girl's life
> easier. They were known as pussy-boys, galboys, fuckboys, and all
> had taken girls' names like Betty, Fifi, Dotty, etc., and were
> universally referred to as "she" and "her."

The inmates' view of the femininity of the queens is shown in another example given by Blake: "Fraulein was standing in the prison yard one day drinking a Coke, surrounded by swains. One of them whispered something in her ear, and Fraulein, who made a mad pretense of chastity, took umbrage, and hurled the drink in his face." According to the viewer, "Dripping, spluttering, he blurted, 'If you wasn't a broad I'd stomp yuh!' "[39]

Blake found that queens and punks were not always notorious, many lived quietly throughout the prison population, only the more overt and flamboyant were segregated in the G-5 cell. Being too overt brought bizarre consequences, such as the following incident about the "Queen of the Rock."[40]

> A really beautiful faggot, was Bobby — a feral, venal, coldly
> poised and enameled creature who filled me with awe. It was said
> that she extracted staggering prices from her lovers for her favors.
>
> One Saturday afternoon, Bobby and her current lover were
> discovered flagrante in an upstairs two-man cell, and taken to the
> Rock Lieutenant, known to cons as Uncle Ben. An old, weary,
> bored, sardonic Cracker, his legendary profanity was said to scorch
> the eyebrows and sear the brain. He could have sent the guilty
> pair to the Flat-Top, the sinister building where the rebellious

were methodically starved. Instead, he procured a chain six feet
long and fastened one end around Bobby's ankle, the other around
the ankle of her lover, saying: "You so goddam fond uh one
anothah, ah'm gonna give you a chance to get fondah." For two
weeks they went around the joint chained together. Their arrival
in Mess Hall was always eagerly awaited. Bobby would come in
the door, the chain looped around her wrist, the crestfallen lover
following like a sullen bear. Then she would drop the chain with a
loud clank on the concrete floor and sweep regally down the aisle
to the steam tables.

Aside from the rather forthright payments to the queens and the
providing of goods and favors to the punks, there is another form of underground economic activity that springs from sexual behavior. In addition to the
lover's payments to the beloved, a semi-permanent affair, or "marriage,"
requires the close priximity of the two persons involved. This need sometimes
sets off a whole chain of economic activity in order to get a man's cellmate
moved out to another location and to get the man's sexual partner moved
into the cell with him. Since inmates control much of the clerical work in the
prison, this shifting of living quarters can generally be accomplished straight-
away if the right people are paid off.

Alcohol
Inside the walls, or outside, men tell one another of great feats of
alcohol consumption. Simple forms of alcoholic beverages are relatively easy
to manufacture and making home brew is a common form of illicit activity in
prisons. At times when inmates are especially active in producing homemade
alcoholic beverages, prison guards express the thought that the place is "about
to float away." As a contraband item in the sub rosa system, the production
of alcohol involves several types of economic activity: assembly of raw
materials, manufacturing, warehousing, distribution, and consumption.

The following account, from *The Riot* by Frank Elli, illustrates
how these multi-faceted activities can be accomplished despite surveillance by
officers:[41]

Cully's next move hinged on the hoped-for sound or movement
which would distract the tower guard behind him, a beefy-faced
man in goggle-sized sunglasses with a rifle in his hands and a pistol
on his side. The moment the guard turned his head, a nod from
one of the men on the roof would send Cully into action. Twenty
feet away, stashed in the window well below the bakery, was a
two-gallon jug full of day-old potato beer. In a matter of seconds,
after the guard turned his head, the jug would be in the empty tar
bucket and, via the block and tackle suspended from the roof, on
its way to consumption above and beyond the eyes of the gun

tower guard . . . . the roof-tarring gang would spend the morning under the blazing sun . . . where the four of them could get peacefully and groggily sick on green potato beer. Anything to break the gnawing monotony.

This fictitious account demonstrates the intricacies of illicit economic activity involving a manufacturing process. While more often than not the actual manufacturing techniques are uncomplicated, great effort is required to conceal the acts of gathering the ingredients, finding a hiding place that will not be discovered before fermentation can occur, and distributing the product among the final consumers.

Inmates are most ingenious in finding ways to simplify the manufacturing process—to reduce production to its basic essentials. The fewer steps necessary, the more economical the operation in that discovery is less likely. Production technology appears to advance and improve as new techniques are developed. The example from *The Riot* employs an old and awkward technology; the ingredients are mixed together in a bucket and the bucket must be concealed for several days while waiting for fermentation to take place. This waiting period is risky because the guards may discover and destroy the product and take disciplinary action against the owners of the brew. Furthermore, another inmate may discover the hiding place and expropriate the product for himself or, if he is a rat, disclose the location to the staff by means of a kite (anonymous note).

An improved technology is being used in Alabama State Prisons. Inmates obtain small, flexible containers—a prophylactic or a plastic bag is suitable. The ingredients—some water, sugar, fruit, and yeast—are sealed in the bag. A man sleeps with the bag between his legs and his body heat hastens the fermentation. This simplified process is faster and involves less risk of discovery.

For the most part, the alcoholic beverages produced are abominable. The inmates who drink usually get sick; nonetheless, for a short time they are able to forget where they are and how much longer they must stay. Clemmer says that the inmate tendency to overindulge causes them to be noticed quickly because they are either drunk or sick. He notes that the officers are less upset by drinking than they are by some other rule infractions. The officers tend to feel that the inmates are justified in getting drunk.[42]

Guards have another rationalization for not harshly judging inmates who make alcohol. They express the belief that when alcohol production and consumption are at a high level in the prison, the use of drugs decreases. We know of no evidence that would tend to validate that viewpoint and suspect that it is a bit of wishful thinking, as the officers believe that drug use is a greater threat to the security of the institution.

Drugs

One category of commodities circulated may be loosely termed "drugs." Since we have placed alcohol in a category of its own, we will define "drugs" as any substance other than alcohol that has some effect on the mental state of inmates. In some cases these substances are grimly effective and in other cases the "mental condition" obtained from using the substance is purely imaginary. In the imaginary category, we had occasion to be familiar with the operation of a local jail in Texas. The jail inmates in this particular location developed the practice of crushing aspirin and mixing it with their smoking tobacco. They eagerly spread the myth that this aspirin-tobacco mixture produced a mild "high." Out of curiosity, we tried it ourselves; but in our skeptical frame of mind could determine no discernible effect. In the ghastly real category, inmates in Alabama prisons are known to shoot lighter fluid in their veins. The result is gruesome. In some cases, the lighter fluid produces intoxication and, in roughly the same number of cases, the lighter fluid results in a horrid death.

Drugs used in prisons include those commonly available in illegal channels outside of the prison, such as amphetamines, barbiturates, narcotics, and hallucinogens. These drugs are sold in prisons much as they are on the streets–dealers find channels into the institution through corrupt guards or outsiders, for instance local merchants, who have access to the prison because of deliveries. Other substances are available in the prison supplies as items not ordinarily consumed as drugs: gasoline, fire extinguisher fluids, lighter fluid, kitchen spices, and glue are examples.

Thomas, in describing his stay in Comstock State Prison, illustrates some of the variety of druglike supplies used and comments on their individual qualities in the following excerpt.[43]

> And we dealt for almost anything, partly out of a desire for the stuff and partly to beat the system. Goof balls, benzedrine, phenobarbitals, splits, and green money floated around regularly. At Sing Sing we had had whiskey, too, but at Comstock I never saw any whiskey, bonded stuff, I mean. Instead we had fermented prunes, fruit wines, and strained shellac—all homemade, of course, but they packed a kick. Some shellac killed one con with a promising career as a sax musician and blinded two others.
>
> Splits were common. They're round white pills with a groove across the middle, some sort of tranquilizer. If you swallow one with a glass of hot water, you get a gone high that's almost like what you get with heroin. We also dealt for red capsules of phenos, two of which, with hot water, produce a forgetting high, and for cooking mace or cinnamon, a large tablespoon of which, with a glass of hot water, closes your eyelids with a way-up-and-out feeling. Sometimes the trusties or outside gang brought in wild marijuana, which we cured and dried on the electric light bulb in the cell. But splits were the kick.

The preference for "splits" illustrates the fads in drug use that are found in the culture outside of the prison as well as inside. At various times, different substances are popular in illegal channels partly because of factors which make some drugs more readily available. For instance in the late 1940s and early 1950s nasal inhalers sold in drug stores for about seventy-five cents. The filling consisted of a piece of heavy paper soaked in benzedrine. The filling could easily be removed and soaked in liquid to produce a potent amphetamine drink. These inhalers, being inexpensive, legally obtainable, and readily available, became popular in prisons. The following excerpts from *The Riot* poignantly illustrates their presence in prison.[44]

> He caught a familiar smell—Benny. Three shirtless cons were hunched over a filing cabinet a few feet away. One held a shiv and was slicing up the cigarette-size roll of medicated cotton from a plastic nasal inhaler. . . .
> Cully grimaced and gagged as he swallowed the piece. It burned his throat and left a sickening taste in his mouth. "Where'd you guys score?"
> "Fisk's desk drawer."
> "How many?"
> "A handful, man. All wrapped up in cellophane and sealed with Scotch tape. Fisk must've busted a packhorse."
> "Yesterday," Cully said. "The rumor is that he nailed Shaky Jake's connection comin' in with a load. That old whiskey-nosed bull that used to have the laundry crew.". . .
> He took a sip of steaming coffee, arousing the sickening medi-cated taste in his mouth. Christ, he thought, what a lousy way for a man to get his kicks. He wouldn't give two bits for a ton of the stuff in the free world but if a guy wanted to get off the natural in a zoo like this, he didn't have much choice.

Some drugs may be pilfered from prison hospital supplies by a few inmates privileged to work in such settings. H. Jack Griswold, an inmate sentenced to Menard Penitentiary in the early 1960s, received an assignment to work in the prison hospital. There he learned of the practices of the convict nurses, who stole drugs on a regular basis. He describes with careful detail the pilfering techniques.[45]

> After becoming well acquainted with a few of the con nurses, I learned that it was not uncommon for them to prescribe medicine—yes, even narcotics. And, what was worse, that much of the Demerol, Darvon, Nembutal, and other such medications they prescribed for their patients were in fact used by the nurses themselves. . . .

The cons used a simple but effective dodge to "beat" the screws, who were required to watch them inject Demerol into post operative and cancer patients.

The con nurse, about to order a hundred milligrams of Demerol, would fill a syringe with distilled water and lay it under one end of a three-way-folded face towel. Then, when the screw brought the container of Demerol, the nurse would draw it into another syringe, and in full view of the screw, lay it atop one end of the folded towel that concealed the water-filled syringe. After that, it was simply a matter of flipping the center flap of the folded towel, which exposed the water-filled syringe and concealed the one containing what the cons called "the good shit." This last deft little maneuver was usually effected while another con—the nurse's confederate—attracted the screw's attention briefly with an inane question or off-the-wall remark about the weather.

When the nurse left to give the shot, the confederate removed the towel and the Demerol-filled syringe from the scene. Later, he and the nurse would share the "stuff" and brag to one another about their cunning while the patient suffered from lack of medication.

Few convicts have access to the high quality drugs such as Demerol, Darvon and Nembutal, stolen by the Menard inmate nurses. A more typical example of the prison "high" is shown in this brief conversation between two inmates:" 'I'm straight,' Gasolino boasted. His eyes glittered and his hand sketched a slow dreamy oval in the air. 'What're you straight on?' Chilly asked. 'Lighter fluid?' 'No, man, good stuff. Glue from the furniture factory,' Nunn said."[46]

Gambling

Legends of great gamblers, about their prowess and their infamy, are told among inmates. Estimates are that 15 to 20 percent of all convicts gamble quite regularly and another 20 percent a couple of times a month. As is the case with many other prison activities initiated by inmates, gambling breaks the boredom of their cloistered life.[47] Clemmer found that card games designed for two players were especially popular because cellmates could play the game. Poker games, which required three or more players, were played in dormitories or in the hospital where more than two men could be assembled.[48]

During the season, there is perpetual gambling on baseball with every conceivable type of wager being made on league games. There are bets on individual games, the number of games won per week, per month, or during the entire season. Bets are made on batting averages, the number of games a pitcher will win during the year, or on the strikes and balls of each inning in a particular game. Wagers are also made on or against the prison team.[49] But inmates also bet on such ordinary events as the number of hymns the prison chaplin will call at the Sunday Protestant service.[50] Wagers between cellmates may be organized so that the loser has to clean the cell for a number of days in succession. Stakes in gambling may be food items—the type available in the commissary or regular dining room food. A loser, for example, may give up his Sunday pie for a month because he picked the Giants instead of the Cubs. There is a prison tale that once upon a time a passive homosexual was wagered against a twenty dollar bill.[51] Nonpayment of a debt can have serious consequences for the offender and is recognized as a major cause of violence in prison.

Pornography

While pornography and erotic material does not constitute a major element in the sub rosa economy, prisons do have a recognizable demand for licentious pictures, literature, and song lyrics. While some inmates regard it with disdain, others rather enjoy it, sometimes using it as conceptual and visual aids. Some prison censorship policies forbid any material considered to be erotic. In institutions taking a restrictive stance toward erotic material, a few guards smuggle in such items and some of it is produced by budding poets or blossoming inmate artists. The New York State Special Commission on Attica noted that hand-drawn pornography in Attica was known as "short-heist." If the artist was reasonably good, short-heist was a salable commodity.[52]

Guards who bring in erotic material may do so because of some sympathetic impulse toward women-starved prisoners. When commenting on British prisons, Terence and Pauline Morris said that most of the material brought in by guards was "artistic" rather than pornographic. The items tended to consist of booklets or albums of photographs of young women in various erotic positions—mostly poses of the act of undressing.[53] These researchers report that photographs and erotic literature were circulated among inmates and that small fees were frequently charged in the exchanges.[54]

Much of the pornographic material that circulates in the prison is the work of convict artists and writers, who proudly lend or trade their work for a small favor or a few cigarettes. The public is aware of self-taught convict artists and authors whose talent bridges the prison walls but most of the artistic endeavors are rather poor. The main theme in convict-produced pictures and stories is heterosexual adventures or exploits, although the characters often have unusual physical conditions and appetites. Sex organs are usually drawn out of scale, making the rest of the body seem insignificant. The Morrises tell of an anthology, composed in a prison exercise book, which was confiscated by prison officials. The anthology was comprised of four purple-hued autobiographies of prostitutes. The first story described the seduction, pregnacy, and adoption of prostitution by a young middle class girl, who entered the life primarily for financial reasons. A second story told of a young girl who was captured and tortured by the Gestapo. The experience caused her to have a sexual desire that could only be satisfied by anal intercourse. The final two stories dealt with incest in childhood, which ultimately resulted in the girls turning to prostitution.[55]

Weapons

The following from Sykes's book are some examples of charge slips written by guards in the New Jersey State Prison. "Possession of home-made shiv sharpened to razor edge on his person and possession of 2 more shivs in cell." The details provided by the officer were: "When inmate was sent to 4 Wing Officer H found 3" steel blade in pocket. I ordered Officer M to search his cell and he found 2 more shivs in process of being sharpened." A complaint by Officer I stated: "Assault with knife on inmate K. During Idle Men's mess at approximately 11:10A.M. this man assaulted Inmate K with a home-made knife. Inmate K was receiving his rations at the counter when Inmate B rushed up to him and plunged a knife in his chest, arm, and back." On the same day Officer L reported: "Fighting and possession of home-made shiv. Struck first blow to Inmate P. He struck blow with a roll of black rubber rolled up in his fist. He then produced a knife made out of wire tied to a tooth brush."[56]

The presence of weapons in prisons creates tension and insecurity for inmates and guards alike. John Irwin interviewed an inmate who told him about his first impression of Soledad Prison and his overwhelming feeling of fear: "The first day I got to Soledad I was walking from the fish tank to the mess hall and this guy comes running down the hall past me, yelling, with a knife sticking out of his back. Man, I was petrified. I thought, what the fuck kind of place is this?"[57] Another new inmate, in another prison, at another time, reports a similar experience. Bill Sands tells about one of his vivid early memories of the use of weapons at San Quentin Prison.[58]

> After two weeks I was still a fish—newcomer or greenhorn. Just before evening lockup, the cons—all of *us* cons—were in the Main Yard, when right in front of me, not more than three feet away, a prison jacket suddenly descended over a man's head and, quick as a snake's tongue, a shiv arced in a semicircle around the man, plunged deep, ripped upward and left him kicking, gurgling and half-disemboweled at my feet. The shiv clattered to the pavement and was kicked aside. I was left there, staring into the eyes of the man who had done it. In a twinkling he had mixed with the crowd. I was too dumbfounded to do likewise. I felt all alone in the big prison yard.

Many prison officials keep an assortment of confiscated prison-made weapons in a showcase close to the central office. Visitors to the prison are shown the collection and get a fair idea of the remarkable diversity of homemade weapons that it is possible to produce within the sub rosa economy. The collection will contain more shivs (knives) than anything else, but some of the lethal-looking knives are big enough to be swords. The weapons made within an institution reflect the characteristics of that particular prison. For example, in the Holman Unit, the maximum security prison in Alabama, the collection of weaponry in a display case in the warden's office has knives with blades that are made of pieces of steel obviously taken from the farm equipment used by the inmates to cultivate the surrounding fields. Many of the knife handles are made by wrapping the metal with the bright colored and distinctive tape used by the license plate shop located within the institution. The farms and the license plate shops at the Holman Unit provide the principal work assignments for the inmates and, inadvertently, the raw materials for the manufacture of these weapons. Within the past year, several inmates in Holman and one guard have been killed with inmate weapons.

The raw materials pilfered for such weapons do not enter the prison because of careless custody procedures. At the Holman Unit, the prisoners returning from work in the fields enter the institution single file through a rear door. In full view of the guards, these prisoners strip off the uniforms that they have worn in the fields and proceed naked through the showers to a point where they draw clean uniforms. This procedure is specifically designed to prevent contraband from entering the prison; yet, the collection of weapons clearly shows that the inmates are ingenious enough to smuggle in material for weapons manufacture despite these procedures.

Robert Neese photographed a collection of these confiscated weapons while he was an inmate in the Iowa State Prison at Fort Madison. The collection of knives and hooks also has two realistic looking pistols, which would be extraordinary useful for escape attempts. Providing background on the manufacture of the weapons, Neese notes that more than 200 hours of labor went into production of one of the pistols; both pistols were carved out of wood with razor blades. The knives in the collection were made from scraps of metal smuggled out of the prison shop and whetted on concrete floors.[59] Weaponry is a skilled craft even (or, especially) in prison.

It is Sykes who points out that the rather large number of weapons in the prison are intended mainly for use by inmates against one another.[60] Demand for weapons is derived from the insecurity and outright fear experienced when living among the varied violence-prone characters in a prison community. A San Quentin inmate describes the pressure of fear after he elected to become an informer in an attempt to get moved to another prison as a result of a threat from a gang of prison toughs. Unable to get the prison officials to move him after informing, he tells of how he survived for the next few weeks. He kept his back to the wall when eating in the mess hall or when taking a shower. He did not attend a movie unless he could persuade a friend to sit behind him and he stayed within sight of a gun-tower when he went out in the yard. He recalls that, although once considered a heavy sleeper, he began to become wide awake each time his cellmate moved during the night.[61]

Summary

This section of the chapter has dealt with self-producers and reciprocal trade. The economic activity described thus far has been geared toward transactions wherein an individual enhances his standard of living by producing commodities for his own use or else engages in barter to obtain services to improve his lot. We have thus far concentrated upon a *consumer* view of the sub rosa economic system. Virtually all inmates engage in some of the activities described in this section. The focus will now be changed to a different vantage point: the profit oriented activites of the inmate entre-preneur.

ENTREPRENEURS AND PROFIT

As is found in developing economies throughout the world, nonessential and sometimes essential economic activities that are degraded or forbidden by the culture are performed by outsiders or groups not bound by the customs of the society. The literature of economic development abounds with examples of groups of people who have played important economic roles because they have not been restricted by the cultural mores—for instance, Indians in Africa, Chinese in Southwest Asia, and Jews in Medieval Europe.

The man called the "merchant" is the prison's entrepreneur—a genuine businessman operating in a world of scarcity. He behaves in much the same way any American entrepreneur would be expected to behave with a similar market structure. However, the convict code operates to deny him status if he is too overtly mercenary. Sykes and Messinger believe that, "The term *merchant* or *peddler* is applied to the inmate who exploits his fellow captives not by force but by manipulation and trickery, and who typically sells or trades goods that are in short supply."[62]

Sykes and Messinger tend to draw sharp distinctions between the low prestige role of the merchant and the high prestige role of the inmate leader, or real man. But as we pointed out earlier, the two roles cannot be kept entirely separate and distinct. It appears to us that the inmate leader is a more subtle and successful entrepreneur than the enterpriser who is branded with the label "merchant."

While the inmate leader operates some of his rackets through henchmen, he is, nonetheless, a vital part of the sub rosa activity. The astute inmate leader who exploits his fellow prisoners by selling goods in short supply maintains admiration and respectability by sharing his profits with his clique. Thus he fulfills the values of the inmate code by sharing in a system of balanced reciprocity. One must bear in mind that the prison community possesses many inmate leaders who control and lead small cliques. Furthermore, the prison community is racially divided. For example, within one prison, white inmates may have a number of cliques, the black inmates may have separate cliques, and inmates descended from Spanish-speaking peoples may have a third group of cliques.

The inmate code described by Sykes applies *within* cliques. If a clique operates a racket under the direction of its inmate leader, the code is not being violated—the inmate leader would not sell goods in short supply to his friends. Inmates may claim that the inmate code is a long chain that binds them together, but it is more often a number of short chains that bind cliques together. One inmate expresses the thought in this way: "The inmate code is enforced by the inmates themselves but enforced in a quite arbitrary kind of way. Everybody cheats to win."[63]

In reality, the inmate social system is the only way that most inmates can achieve success and leadership in the inmate community. Malcolm Braly's novel, *On The Yard,* is the story of a young man in prison who is obviously *both* an inmate leader and a merchant. The character Chilly Willy is an inmate leader because he has a clique of followers, and he is a "merchant" because his economic exploits constitute a convict Horatio Alger success story. It appears that the merchant designation described by Sykes and Messinger applies to the convict loner who is so greedy that he tries to peddle his wares to everyone around him without a "balanced reciprocity of sharing" with his friends. But for the present let us drop this philosophical hassle and concentrate on the behavior of the prison entrepreneur and, for the sake of simplicity, refer to him as the merchant.

The following example from Braly's story, which focuses on the notorious Chilly Willy, illustrates several facets of a merchant's operations.

> "Chilly had hit the big yard broke at twenty-three. He had borrowed enough to subscribe to a national sports sheet . . . he had won far more than he had lost. A steady flow of cigarettes had moved into his hands, but they had proved an inconvenience and he had decided to put them to work."[64]

The account illustrates a pattern that one could as easily observe in the outside society. Chilly found a way to earn money in the economic channels available to him. Being a shade more innovative and successful than the average man, Chilly gradually accumulated some financial capital. At that point, he decided that his idle financial capital was not productive and he should use it to establish himself in a business. The business he selected was drug peddling. He carefully cultivated a staff member who worked as a mail room clerk. Once he decided that Harmon was vulnerable, he began to bribe him with currency (bought in the sub rosa system with cigarettes). Chilly eventually was able to induce the man to smuggle drugs into the prison. The quotation below shows how such an operation can be managed, how henchmen can be employed to do the dirty work, and how profitable the enterprise can be.[65]

> These inhalers of various brands were packed with an average of three hundred milligrams of amphetamine sulphate or some similar drug with the same properties, and retailed in any drugstore for seventy-five cents. Harmon was paid two dollars for each tube he smuggled in, and Chilly, without ever touching them, turned them over to his front man in the gym.
>
> At this point the inhalers were cracked open and the cottons in which the active drug was suspended were removed. It was tacitly understood that if a tube were cut into thirds, the thirds were sold for halves, and if it were cut into fourths, the fourths were sold for thirds, on down to tenths which were actually fifteenths. Such a fifteenth, wrapped in wax paper, was sold for either three dollars soft money or a carton of cigarettes. The profit was approximately thirty-five dollars on a single inhaler.

There are some salient points in this description of drug trade. Harmon, the mail room clerk, was a low paid employee who was relatively easy to bribe to bring in the first few inhalers in his lunch box. Once he began to smuggle, he was at the mercy of Chilly, who could with a word here and there cause him to lose his job. While soft money was contraband in the prison being described, it did flow in regularly. The wives and girl friends of the inmates slipped soft money to their males on visiting days. The inmates who received this contraband were able to avoid detection when they were searched after these visits by hiding the money in the vicinity of their genitals where the guards were reluctant to feel during a personal search.[66] Thus the mechanisms being described in the quotation illustrate how two types of contraband are fed into the sub rosa economic system of the prison from the free world. The custody measures of the prison were just lax enough to allow a steady flow of inhalers and currency into the system. The character in the example, through his successful and expanding business activities, had managed to corner a goodly amount of the contraband currency entering the system.[67]

> By convict standards he was a millionaire. In various places throughout the institution he had approximately three hundred cartons of cigarettes. Several men who had reputations for holding big stuff were little more than the managers of one of Chilly's

warehouses. He never exposed their floor shows. They took heat off him and when occasionally they were busted and the cigarettes lost to confiscation, Chilly accepted it as a business reverse. If he cornered every butt in the joint and a year of futures he still wouldn't have anything, but the slower and more difficult accumulation of soft money could some day mean something. In the hollow handle of the broom leaning carelessly in the corner of his cell he had a roll of bills totaling close to a thousand dollars. If the Classification Committee became careless he might get a chance to use it.

This latter illustration shows how much of the economic activity could be handled by henchmen and lieutenants, who probably were tagged with the "merchant" argot role described by Sykes and Messinger. And these examples give some understanding of the entrepreneur's motivation and his techniques.

The previous section of the chapter gave some insight into the types of goods and services available in the sub rosa system. However, the previous section concentrated on self-producers and reciprocal trade. At this point we shall systematically consider some of the goods and services suitable for methodical profit making by the prison merchant.

Food

In a previous example we noted that weapons take on some of the characteristics of the prison industry, e.g., weapons being made from materials stolen from the work shops. Food follows a similar pattern. The Draper Correctional Center in Alabama has, as one of its main work tasks, the function of truck farming to provide fresh vegetables for its own population and for other state prisons in the system. During the season for fresh vegetables, prison merchants are known to systematically market tomato sandwiches late at night. One would not suppose that the prisoners in this institution are more fond of tomatoes than are other inmates, rather the nature of the institution is such that bread and tomatoes can be pilfered more readily than other types of food.

Consider, for clarification, a completely different prison in a different part of the country where the inmate merchants regularly marketed burritos. The burritos are made in the prison bakery and "packed" out to the cell blocks for retailing by the prison merchants. In a story called "Too Much Integrity," Larry Harsha tells about conflict with a guard who is on the verge of disrupting the regularity of the sales operation. This example of food retailing shows the difficult circumstances of marketing a product with regularity. A constant ability to deceive and distract guards is necessary as well as an ability to conceal items on one's person in such a way so that they are not detected.[68]

I break down to the bakery. Yeah, they're knocking out big-time burritos! When I get there they've got them lined up on the table and we start bagging up the ones for me to take to the block; five bags, five burritos to a bag. I've got some time to kill so we're just standing around talking shit when Perkins comes in looking for a burrito. He gets to eyeballing them bags and since this guy hates everybody, there ain't no telling what he's liable to do. So I figure I'd better turn this asshole and get rid of him. Now, the easiest way to turn this guy is to start capping on him; he'll get hot and put it in the wind. . . .

And it works! He gets hot, but he don't know what to say, so he mouths off some weak shit and heads for the kitchen.

Now that he's gone I figure I better get my shit and get in the wind, so I get four bags in my shirt and I'm gonna pack the fifth one in my mitt. I get my jacket set on my shoulders so you can't tell I'm loaded unless you're checking me out in profile, and even then you can't be sure.

The demand for illicit food marketed on a regular basis stems largely from the schedule of the prison. Prisons run on a tight and early schedule. A large prison controls its inmates partly by the "divide and conquer" technique, by handling the prisoners in small groups so not too many are together at one time. Different cell blocks will be sent to the dining hall at different times. The effect is that dining begins early in the day; the first shift of prisoners may arrive at the dining hall for breakfast at 5 A.M. After several shifts of prisoners have received breakfast, there is only a short pause in the dining room activity before the early shift returns for lunch. The same process is repeated in the afternoon. All inmates have been fed three meals by approximately five in the afternoon. There is a long and hungry time between dinner and breakfast, especially for those inmates eating on the early shift. During the evening hours most of the inmates are confined to their cells or dormitories, so if they are to purchase any food through the illicit economic system, it must be delivered to them by those relatively few inmates who are not closely confined. In the last example, the burrito merchant was free to go to the bakery because he had just finished a tour of duty.

Any product will command a price if it is scarce and has utility. Air has utility, but is plentiful and "free." Garbage is plentiful, but has negative utility—one is willing to pay to get rid of it. Diamonds have little actual utility, especially when compared with water, but diamonds are scarce and command a high price because of their scarcity. People buy diamonds partly because they are expensive. Frequently, commodities have time and place utility. The food sold in the evening hours has these latter characteristics. The tomato sandwiches and the burritos in the examples given probably could not be marketed in the prison during the daylight hours when the meals are close together. These food products have time utility at night, when the inmates are hungry, and place utility if they are delivered to the cells. A letter written by an inmate of Folsom Prison illustrates that even hot water has time and place utility during the long hours of the night. His letter expresses regret that everyone is locked up so tightly that he cannot even buy a cup of hot water for coffee even though he is willing to pay a package of cigarettes and has the other necessary ingredients.[69]

Thus it would appear that the merchants who can deliver any kind of edible food to the locked-in prisoners during the evening hours provide both time and place utility for which the customers are willing to pay. The inmates that we have interviewed about such food sales seem to recognize that an essential service is performed and they do not express resentment toward the "profiteering" of these merchants.

Gambling

Gambling may be organized by prison entrepreneurs so that it becomes a racket instead of a pastime between two inmates. Inmates who engage in gambling in a systematic manner are, in effect, bookies. They operate a business for a profit—not unlike the managers of the Las Vegas casinos. The main character in Braly's *On the Yard*, Chilly Willy, conducted his gambling operations as follows.[70]

> Chilly was beginning to take a few bets. He was currently
> booking football. In the winter he booked basketball and in the
> spring and summer baseball. When the tracks were running he
> booked horses. He was prepared to make some bet on any fight,
> national or local, or any other sports event except marble tourna-
> ments and frog jumping contests. He felt he did well.

Describing a prison's top gambler, John Irwin and Donald R. Cressey noted that the man was always taking bets on all types of sporting events and that cartons of cigarettes could always be found in his cell despite the fact that he did not smoke.[71] The particular inmate being described had two rackets. He was a worker in a laundry room, which allowed him to charge inmates a fee if they wanted special laundering; and since he came into contact with many inmates in the course of his laundry duties, it was easy for him to take bets. At times he took his fees in "favors" in order to be able to influence inmates in key jobs who could arrange cell and job changes.[72]

Loan Sharking and Bad Debts

Loan sharking, a common form of prison enterprise, is a conve-
nient way to become a merchant. The rate of interest is surprisingly standard and recognizable to anyone who has ever spent time around a military unit or borrowed money from a loan shark in a ghetto. The interest rate is "three for

two" and the life of the loan is "until pay day." The loan and the interest rate in the prison differ from the outside world only in that the prison loan is made with cigarettes instead of with money. The process is illustrated in Braly's descriptive novel by an inmate who is expecting to receive a gift of money from his aunt on the outside and decides to borrow a carton of cigarettes with the expectation that he will be able to pay it back when his present arrives. This inmate, Juleson, goes to the prison merchant, Chilly Willy (whose real name is Oberholster). The transaction is conducted as follows.[73]

> "Oberholster, can I borrow a box at three-for-two?"
> "Maybe. Which draw will you pay on?"
> "The second draw in December. That's about a month."
> "That's right. Did you learn lightning calculation in there?" Chilly indicates the ed building.
> Juleson smiled. "How about it?"
> "Sure, three-for-two's my game. What kind you want?"
> "Camels."
> "Come on up to the gym, I'll get them for you."

Unfortunately, Juleson did not receive the money that he was expecting, could not pay the debt on time, and found it necessary to tell Chilly that he could not pay. The following example illustrates why the practice of loan sharking is so vicious whether it is conducted inside or outside of the prison. The already exorbitant rate of interest compounds rapidly when payment is delayed and the loan shark begins coercive threats to intimidate the victim. This is illustrated in Juleson's case as follows.[74]

> "You got my stuff?" Chilly asked, automatically falling into the tone and vocabulary he used for these exchanges.
> "Well, no, as a matter of fact I haven't. That's what I wanted to see you about." . . .
> "All right, when do I get my stuff?"
> Juleson shrugged, meeting Chilly's level gaze with difficulty. "To be honest with you, I don't know."
> "You be honest. That's a keen virtue. But I can't smoke it, and I can't pay the people I owe with it. How much you figure you'll owe me next month?"
> "Why fifteen packs, a box at three-for-two. That's right, isn't it?"
> "No, that isn't right," Chilly repeated with satirical patience.
> "You had *one* month to get up fifteen packs. Now it's twenty-two packs. Another month and it's three cartons. Are you following me?"

Juleson's troubles are serious at this point. There are no legal remedies for bad debts either inside or outside the prison because loan sharking is illegal. In order for loan sharks to operate successfully—that is, if they are to expect their customers to pay them—they must have a debt collection mechanism which is effective. The mechanism used is sheer force. Somewhat later in Braly's story, we find that Chilly has lost his regular debt collector and is contracting with another dangerously unbalanced inmate to beat up Juleson. Chilly knows that he cannot "write off" any bad debts if he is to remain in business. The debt collection contract goes like this.[75]

> Stick approached Chilly for the second time in the morning before work call. Chilly, noting that this kid looked even stranger in full daylight, took him aside to ask, "How bad do you want on that gym list?"
> Stick answered as he had the day before, "It's important."
> "You Vampires do any collection work?"
> "We can."
> "All right. I got a guy I want whipped on. You do the job and you're on the night gym list."
> "How bad?"
> "I want him to know he's been worked on. You don't have to kill him."
> "That's worth a little more than a gym assignment."
> "You want to bargain?"
> "No. Okay, who is it?"
> "Come on, I'll point him out."

Despite the dangers of borrowing money from loan sharks, there is considerable demand for loans. Juleson, the victim in the preceding illustrations, fell into his trap because of a psychological factor economists call "low time preference." Simply stated, low time preference means that a person has difficulty waiting for the pleasures of consumption. In our society of easy down payments and consumer debt, we are not at all unfamiliar with the phenomena; it is common. Yet a few people in the American society, and some peoples in various parts of the world at various times in history, have managed to develop high time preferences. High time preference seems to be a trait that is learned by living in a society where the cultural values place emphasis upon the value of self-discipline.

For example, Britain developed traditions of high time preference among its upper classes during the eighteenth and nineteenth centuries. The upper classes valued the status of living on interest. One generation would pass along an inheritance to the following generation, but the inheritance was always invested. The heirs lived on the income from the investment and would have been horrified at the suggestion that they might spend some of the principal. Status from living on the interest from investments was reinforced by remarking to one's peers that, "of course, we never go into capital." In many cases, the income from such inherited investment was modest and the temptation to spend the principal was too much to resist for some young men. Those who fell into this temptation—those who expressed a low time preference—were considered to be "rotters." For those who resisted the urge to spend the capital, the satisfactions derived from the status awarded to those who "lived on income" outweighed the satisfactions of spending the family fortune on consumption.

In our society, high interest rates and compounding of interest on overdue debts seem somehow to be morally wrong. In fact one finds many state laws which make "usury" a crime. Usury is the act of charging an interest rate that is too high, but exactly what constitutes being "too high" is generally decided rather arbitrarily and without reference either to economic principles or implications. Interest, as other income, is *earned* income. The lender performs a valid and useful service for his customers and for society as a whole. The lender furnishes time utility to the borrower, who is willing to pay a fee (interest) for the use of purchasing power. This fee for time preference might be rather modest if the lender is virtually certain that the money will be repaid when due. But the lender cannot be certain, and because of this lack of certainty the lender incurs "risk." Some loans are, on the surface, more risky than others. The lender adds increments to the basic "time preference" fee to compensate for the risk involved. Consequently, different interest rates are charged for different loans to different groups.

Loaning money on a military post, in a ghetto, or in a prison is highly risky—it is even more risky than it might otherwise be when laws or institution rules forbid the practice and effectively block any legal remedy for bad debts. When a debt is overdue, the risk of forfeiture is even greater; hence, the compounding of interest to compensate for the increased risk. Under these high risk conditions, the interest rate charged in prison is not high compared to the interest rate charged carefully selected bank customers. The same economic behavior can be observed in international finance. Developing countries trying to attract financial capital are regarded as extremely risky places to put capital because of the unstable political climate. It is not uncommon to find exorbitant interest rates in these countries.

Protection

Protection is included in the "services" category of the goods and services supplied by inmate merchants. An inmate author explains the protection racket and how the demand for protection develops. Lamson describes commissary day in the prison and the vulnerability of what he calls easy victims—the old, the weak, the feeble, the simple, and the cowardly.[76]

> The men come out of the office well loaded with gunny sacks and pasteboard cartons. One thus burdened with riches runs some risk in the course of his journey back to his cell, if his way leads

through a remote or deserted part of the prison. Like the traveller of medieval times, he may be set upon by a robber band, his baggage plundered, and himself threatened or even beaten.

According to Lamson, hijackery, mugging, and robbery with violence are not as frequent as extortion (forcing the inmate to buy protection). The extortion technique is simply more functional than robbery. Lamson explains the extortion racket as follows.[77]

> In forcing the pay-off for protection, the gangster follows the same technique as his brothers on the outside. The victim is warned that he is in danger of being hi-jacked by some unnamed mob; but that for so many sacks of weed a month his friend the gangster will save him from harm. Since the gangsters choose their victims with care, selecting only the more spineless and helpless of the cons, this threat usually suffices. If a man should refuse to pay, or if he squeals, he will likely be knifed or slugged quietly, which not only settles his case but has an excellent moral effect on the other suckers.

The protection illustration given above is not so much a service as it is a nonbarter type of transfer of wealth. Other similar transfers are theft, gifts, robbery, and blackmail. These are similar to transfer payments in the free world economy, which constitute a form of income redistribution wherein no economic value is created. However, in some cases protection is a valid service. Sykes described the "gorilla" as an inmate social type who makes prison life especially dangerous and insecure because he takes the goods and services that he wants from other inmates by force.[78] An inmate may actually need to be protected from some predatory individual or group. He may buy protection within the inmate culture in order to avoid seeking help from the prisoner staff—an act that would cause him to be labeled as a rat.

The social types in the passive homosexual role, such as the punks and the queens, are especially in need of protection from the aggressive jocker types. This protection is obtained by attaching themselves to someone with the power to protect them. Chilly Willy, Braly's main character, carefully explains this to a "queen" who has been placed in his two-man cell and who he plans to have transferred to the cell of one of his henchmen.[79]

> "Your friend. Red. I don't like him."
>   "He's all right."
>   "And you're just going to give me to him? What do you think I am?"
>   Chilly stared levelly. "All right, what are you?"
>   "I'm a person. You can't take that away from me. I'm a person."

"I'm not trying to take anything away from you. Listen, you silly little bitch, this is *not* Tracy. If someone doesn't stand in front of you, you'll get your little ass killed, or someone will be ripping you off every time you try to take a shower. Not that I give a damn one way or another, but Red says he wants you, and that's good enough for me. No one, and I mean *no one*, is going to mess with what's Red's, because that's the same as messing with me.

Miscellaneous Goods and Services

The New York State Special Commission on Attica conducted a comprehensive investigation of the September 1971 prison riot. The Commission begins its massive report with several chapters on prison conditions in general and the conditions in Attica prison specifically. Some space is devoted to the sub rosa economic activity (called "hustling") at Attica. The entrepreneurial activities at Attica include all those activities discussed above and more. A brief discussion of the forms of hustling at Attica will give some indication of the wide diversity of sub rosa economic behavior.

The Commission found that some 500 inmates at Attica were enrolled in correspondence courses where the textbook was drawn and the inmate studied the lessons in his cell. Papers were graded by an inmate. Since the inmates believed that the parole board would consider their success in the courses to be a sign of rehabilitation, a racket had developed around the grading of papers. Inmates teachers received cigarettes and other bounty for awarding passing grades.[80]

Attica inmates were issued a rather scant supply of toilet articles and were allowed to shower but once a week. Nevertheless, the rules of the institution required them to be clean. Inmates were forced to wash their own socks and non-issue clothing in the sinks in their cells. And these sinks have only cold water. A water boy brought two quarts of hot water to each cell in the afternoon or evening. Because of the difficulty of obtaining enough hot water to keep clean, a racket was operated by the opportunistic water boys, who would sell extra pails of hot water to the prisoners in their cells.[81]

Attica used an inmate for a librarian. Inmates were forced to pay the librarian to obtain popular books.[82] The demand for literature with a sexual content and the operation of this type of racket is illustrated in *On The Yard.*[83]

Chilly chose his reading material from the select books that never saw light on the mainline shelves, but were hidden in the back room as a rental library operated by the head inmate librarian, who charged from a pack to five packs a week depending upon the demand for a specific book. Most of these books were L and L's, derived from Lewd and Lascivious Conduct, hotdog books heavy with sex, and they were always in demand. But unless they were brand-new, most of the L and L books in the institution had suffered a specific mutilation. An unwary reader would pursue a slow and artfully constructed fictional seduction, feeling the real and tightening clutch of his own excitement, turn the page and fall into an impossible aberration of context. He would discover several pages missing, sliced out of the book so neatly it was difficult to detect even when the pages numbers clearly indicated they were gone, and almost impossible to detect before actually reading the book.

Presently, one is able to identify a number of militant political groups who have members both inside and outside of the prisons. The inmates who belong to organizations that issue literature will frequently desire access to those publications. If it is banned by the prison censors, as it sometimes is, a demand for the material arises in the illicit channels and is supplied in various ways. Russel G. Oswald, in writing his personal account of the Attica riot, discusses some of the activities of militant prisoners in the state system. The following excerpts are statements by inmates in the Auburn Penitentiary who are responding to interview questions of staff members.[84]

> "Radical magazines such as *Panther E* and *Mohammed Speaks* ought to be banned. They won't let *Mein Kampf* in here."
> "Militant literature is smuggled into the institution by visitors and some staff members."
> "Militants get all their support from the streets, from lawyers and other supporters. They correspond with unauthorized individuals through the new sealed-letter procedure. All the writer does is indicate he is writing to an attorney. The letter is not opened."

Another possibility for entering the activity of the sub rosa economic system is found in the services area. Inmates who spend years studying law books in the prison library eventually become capable lawyers, who, after achieving a local reputation, are able to sell their services in the illicit system. The possibility is depicted in the following passage from the Attica Commission report.[85]

> There is a breed of men in prison known as "inmate lawyers." These are inmates who have no formal training in the law but who have become knowledgeable about decisions of interest to inmates. They assist other inmates in preparing petitions attacking their convictions, and are generally held in great esteem by the population of the institution. There were several such men in Attica in September 1971.

Inmates who are assigned to work in the laundry are in a position to provide special services to other prisoners who are willing to pay for them. The demand for laundry service arises because the prison provides such service too infrequently or because the more prosperous inmates want some frills such as starch in their uniforms, simple modifications to make their uniforms look distinctive, or access to the newer and better uniforms. The laundry hustle is described by the Attica Commission.[86]

> One of the most common hustles involved the laundry. To keep personal articles of clothing clean, many inmates "bought a laundry man" with cigarettes, the most common medium of exchange. An inmate testified: "You usually get a contract with one man and you pay him like maybe a carton of cigarettes every month and he will take care of your laundry for you." Similarly, if an inmate needed a new pair of pants between scheduled clothing issues he made a deal with a contact in the tailor shop or through a middleman.

All the preceding illustrations in this section revolve primarily around economic transactions among inmates. In a few cases, a guard was corrupted and paid to bring contraband into the prison on a regular basis or a friendly guard was persuaded to bring "harmless" contraband, such as erotic material and militant pamphlets, into the prison on an irregular basis.

There is one other type of economic activity that involves the staff members on a regular basis. The social type known as a rat frequently has economic motives for his actions. His impact, in terms of disrupting the flow of economic activity, can be considerable. Sykes distinguishes between rats who reveal their identity to the officials—usually by signing notes sent to officials—and "anonymous" rats, who do not reveal their identity when they send information to the guards. Sykes believes that the main motivation of the rats who reveal their identity is to win preferential treatment from their "rulers" in exchange for information.[87] The anonymous rat may also be economically motivated in that he can rid himself of competitors or settle a grudge by revealing the nature of the operation of some of the prison rackets. Whatever the motivation of a particular rat, he poses a substantial threat to the stability of the system. If rats are active and not controlled by the inmate culture, they can cause several "business losses" and "recessions" in the sub rosa economy.

The two preceding sections have indicated the types of sub rosa economic activity occurring in male prisons—that is, the self-producer/reciprocal trade activity and entrepreneurial activity. The sections have also illustrated the large variety of goods and services by providing descriptive material showing the source of demand for such goods and services and the techniques of manufacture and distribution. Since the extent of illicit economic activity is quite large, the question arises as to the attitudes of the prison staff members, who obviously cannot be unaware of all of this underground activity.

STAFF AND CONTRABAND

Prison guards routinely engage in surveillance of inmates and conduct both personal and cell searches. The custody function of the prison involves more than just keeping the inmates from escaping and maintaining peace within the inmate population; it also means that contraband is to be kept out of the prison. Considering the large amount of illicit economic activity—all of which centers around goods and services (defined as "contraband" simply because they are forbidden)—one wonders how the guards can fail so completely in their assigned chore of eliminating contraband. The answer to this question, as with most, is multifaceted: some guards are corrupt, some guards are sympathetic to the plight of prisoners, and all guards must be pragmatic to survive in their career role. Each of these three facets merit individual consideration.

In a 1969 survey, the Joint Commission on Correctional Manpower and Training found that 36 percent of the line workers in adult institutions made less than $6,000 per year, and an additional 43 percent of these personnel made between $6,000 and $8,000 per year.[88] Such low salaries clearly indicate that there is financial need among these guards, many of whom are the family breadwinners. It is reasonable to suppose that some guards can be corrupted by inmate racketeers who have ready cash. At times, corruption can be blatant, as was discovered by the Nassau County (New York) District Attorney, William Cahn, when he hired undercover agents to investigate jail conditions. The following excerpts relate the corruption uncovered in that institution when twenty members of organized crime were incarcerated in the jail.[89]

> The operatives reported that certain guards not only treated these prisoners with the respect and dignity uniformly denied others but also ingratiatingly provided them with services and favors . . . .
> Liquor and narcotics were supplied to these inmates for a price. Guards delivered contraband letters to the outside for payment of as much as $50 and brought letters back into the jail for these men. The report included one instance in which a top mobster in the group was given a female prisoner for his sexual use. This very same prisoner, who was drunk much of the time, boasted of his special treatment to the other prisoners.

The same report indicates that corrupt guards will engage in economic exploitation of prisoners in indirect ways in addition to taking money from those who have it. Cahn's investigators reported ". . . instances of petty theft by 'pack rat' guards who, having easy access to prison supplies, stuffed their pockets with razor blades or other such articles or wore several pairs of new pants when they left for home." One of the investigators was an eyewitness to the following act: "An officer was ordered to send a set of new underwear to a hospitalized inmate. Deciding that the new underwear was too good for a prisoner, he took off the underwear he was wearing, put on the new underwear meant for the prisoner, and sent his dirty underwear to Meadowbrook Hospital for the inmate."[90]

Oswald's personal story of Attica includes a statement by an Auburn inmate: " 'Several shop foremen will bring in anything for a few bucks. Some guys bring in stuff, trying to be O.K.' "[91] The inmate's statement brings us to the second facet of the staff's reaction to contraband. While some guards are corrupt, others simply want the inmates to consider them to be "nice guys" and bring in contraband that they regard as harmless. Guards are subject to the same social pressures that everyone is subjected to in their daily life. The working conditions of guards puts them into contact with the same groups of inmates during every work day. He gets to know them by name and learns to like some of them and to think of them as his friends. It is natural that the guard occasionally yields to the desire to be accepted and to be liked. The guard's supervisors warn him against such tendencies, but the guards spends more time with inmates than with his supervisors or his fellow line workers.

Sykes, in a section of *The Society of Captives,* describes what he calls "the defects of total power." His explanation is pertinent to the third facet of staff's attitudes toward contraband—that is, the notion that guards are pragmatic. Sykes points out that guards cannot control the inmates by force because the use of force results in reports to his supervisors, reports that call attention to the difficulty that the guard is having in handling his charges. If a guard consistently and frequently draws attention to himself by using physical force or the coercive techniques of having the prisoner's privileges or freedoms reduced, he will soon discover that his supervisors regard him as incompetent. The dilemma of the guard centers on the fact that he has no nonpunitive means of controlling the inmate's behavior because the inmate receives all of his privileges noncontingently soon after he enters the prison. As a pragmatic matter, the guard needs a way to control the behavior of his charges by rewarding them, but he has no legal way to give rewards for desired behavior. Being a practical man, the guard overlooks minor rule infractions such as the possession of some types of contraband. Because it is the only bargaining power that he has, he overlooks these infractions intentionally and, in turn, the inmates allow him to control them to a degree.[92]

Richard Cloward relates an account of some deliberate overlooking of rule infractions by a mess sergeant (staff) concerning his kitchen workers (inmates). The mess sergeant knowingly allowed the kitchen workers to illegally manufacture an alcoholic beverage using ingredients from the mess supplies. In some cases the sergeant supplied the materials himself. The sergeant's motivation was simple: he was responsible for feeding 1,500 men. The only significant reward that he had to offer the inmate workers was this forbidden privilege of making and selling "jack." In return, the inmates worked efficiently and kept the sergeant out of trouble with his superiors.[93]

While the preceding example shows how one staff member bends rules to get a task that he is responsible for accomplished, the following example demonstrates the same technique being used to accomplish the custody task of running a cell block peacefully. An inmate of California's Vacaville candidly tells of falling in love with a homosexual. The classification committee in the institution told the inmate that his lover would be allowed to move into the cell with him. They were to be allowed to have sexual freedom in return for abiding by other prison rules. Both would be placed in isolation if either one broke any other rule.[94]

SUMMARY

Considering the multifaceted reasons for staff ignoring of rule infractions that have been outlined here, it is not surprising that a considerable amount of illicit economic activity can and does occur in the prison community. In the first place, inmates learn to be adept at concealing the sub rosa economic events. In the second place, the prison staff, although aware of a number of infractions, are willing to tolerate them. In this chapter we have considered the events and issues surrounding the sub rosa economic activity as it occurs in male prisons. The material considered here has been largely descriptive. Before applying a theoretical framework to the subject matter, it is appropriate to consider the nature of illicit economic activity in prisons for females. The social structure and, consequently, the nature of the economic transactions, differ significantly in women's institutions. The following chapters consider the differences.

Notes to Chapter 3

1. Gresham M. Sykes, *The Society of Captives* (Princeton, N.J: Princeton University Press, 1971), pp. 66-67.

2. Charles R. Tittle and Drollene P. Tittle. "Social Organization of Prisoners: An Empirical Test," *Social Forces* 43 (December 1964): 216-221.

3. Stanton Wheeler, "Socialization in Correctional Communities," *American Sociological Review* 26 (October 1961): 697-712.

4. Gresham M. Sykes and Sheldon L. Messinger, "The Inmate Social System," *Theoretical Studies in Social Organization of the Prison,* by Richard A. Cloward and others (New York: Social Science Research Council, 1960) pp. 5-19.

5. Clarence Schrag, "Some Foundations for a Theory of Correction," in *The Prison: Studies in Institutional Organization and Change,* ed. Donald R. Cressey (New York: Holt, Rinehart and Winston, 1966) p. 343.

6. Sykes, p. 91.

7. The terminology and concepts used in this analysis of resources were developed by Erich W. Zimmermann, the acknowledged master craftsman of the theory of resources. See: Erich W. Zimmerman, *World Resources and Industries,* rev. ed. (New York: Harper & Row, 1951).

8. Tom Murton and Joe Hyams, *Accomplices to the Crime* (New York: Grove Press, 1970), pp. 46-48.

9. "A necessity is a good for which it is hard to find substitutes," according to Robert L. Heilbroner, *The Economic Problem,* 2nd ed. (Englewood Cliffs, N.J: Prentice-Hall, 1970), p. 442.

10. Howard B. Gill, "A New Prison Discipline: Implementing the Declaration of Principles of 1870," *Federal Probation* 34 (June 1970): 29-33.

11. *Ibid.,* 29.

12. *Ibid.*

13. Sykes, p. 43.

14. Richard H. McCleery, "Authoritarianism and the Belief System of Incorrigibles," in *The Prison,* ed. Donald R. Cressey (New York: Holt, Rinehart and Winston, 1966), p. 264, clearly describes this prison unit.

15. Manning Nash, *Primitive and Peasant Economic Systems* (San Francisco: Chandler, 1966), p. 24.

16. Norman S. Hayner, "Washington State Correctional Institutions as Communities," *Social Forces* 21 (March 1943): 319.

17. Rose Giallombardo, *Society of Women: A Study of a Woman's Prison* (New York: John Wiley, 1966), p. 121.

18. David Lamson, *We Who Are About to Die* (New York: Charles Scribner's Sons, 1936), pp. 223-224.

19. *Ibid.,* pp. 224-225.

20. Donald Clemmer, *The Prison Community* (New York: Holt, Rinehart and Winston, 1968), pp. 167-169.

21. *Ibid.,* p. 168.

22. New York State Special Commission on Attica, *Attica: The Official Report* (New York: Praeger, 1972), p. 190.

23. H. Jack Griswold and others, *An Eye for an Eye* (New York: Pocket Books, 1971), p. 17.

24. John H. Gagnon and William Simon, "The Social Meaning of Prison Homosexuality," *Federal Probation* 32 (March 1968): 25.

25. Peter C. Buffum, *Homosexuality in Prisons* (Washington, D.C: U.S. Government Printing Office, 1972), p. 13.

26. Gagnon and Simon, 23-29.

27. Buffum, p. 15.

28. *Ibid.*

29. *Ibid.,* pp. 9-10.

30. Charles R. Tittle, "Inmate Organization: Sex Differentiation and the Influence of Criminal Subcultures," *American Sociological Review* 34 (August 1969): 499.

31. Eve Pell, ed., *Maximum Security: Letters From Prison* (New York: E. P. Dutton, 1972), p. 43.

32. Piri Thomas, *Down These Mean Streets* (New York: Alfred A. Knopf, 1967), pp. 265-267.

33. Lester Douglas Johnson, *The Devil's Front Porch* (Lawrence, Kan: University Press of Kansas, 1970), pp. 108-109.

34. *Ibid.*

35. Clemmer, p. 261.

36. Griswold, pp. 140-141.

37. *Ibid.*, pp. 136-137.

38. James Blake, *The Joint* (Garden City, N.Y: Doubleday, 1971), pp. 66-67.

39. *Ibid.*, p. 67.

40. *Ibid.*, pp. 67-68.

41. Frank Elli, *The Riot* (New York: Coward, McCann & Geoghegan, 1966), pp. 9-10.

42. Clemmer, p. 243.

43. Thomas, p. 258.

44. Elli, pp. 29-37.

45. Griswold, p. 125.

46. Malcolm Braly, *On the Yard* (Boston: Little, Brown, 1967), p. 89.

47. James V. Bennett, *I Chose Prison* (New York: Alfred A. Knopf, 1970), pp. 26-29.

48. Clemmer, p. 239.

49. *Ibid.*

50. Bennett, pp. 26-29.

51. Clemmer, pp. 238-241.

52. Special Commission on Attica, p. 53.

53. Terence Morris and Pauline Morris, *Pentonville: A Sociological Study of an English Prison* (London: Routledge and Kegan Paul, 1963), pp. 185-186.

54. *Ibid.*, p. 185.

55. *Ibid.*, p. 186.

56. Sykes, pp. 44-45.

57. John Irwin, *The Felon* (Englewood Cliffs, N.J: Prentice-Hall, 1970), p. 69.

58. Bill Sands, *My Shadow Ran Fast* (New York: New American Library, 1964), p. 38.

59. Robert Neese, *Prison Exposures* (Philadelphia: Chilton, 1959), p. 61.

60. Sykes, p. 92.

61. Pell, p. 45.

62. Sykes and Messinger, p. 9.

63. Robert J. Minton, Jr., ed., *Inside: Prison American Style* (New York: Random House, 1971), p. 53.

64. Braly, p. 84.

65. *Ibid.*, p. 85.

66. *Ibid.*, p. 86.

67. *Ibid.*, p. 84.

68. Larry Harsha, "Too Much Integrity," in *Inside: Prison American Style,* ed. Robert J. Hinton, Jr. (New York: Random House, 1971), pp. 61-62.

69. Pell, p. 63.

70. Braly, pp. 83-84.

71. John Irwin and Donald R. Cressey, "Thieves, Convicts and the Inmate Culture," *Social Problems* 10 (Fall 1962): 149.

72. *Ibid.*

73. Braly, p. 91.

74. *Ibid.*, p. 153.

75. *Ibid.*, pp. 247-248.

76. Lamson, p. 227.

77. *Ibid.*, 227-228.

78. Sykes, pp. 90-93.

79. Braly, p. 249.

80. Special Commission on Attica, p. 81.

81. *Ibid.,* p. 42.
82. *Ibid.,* p. 46.
83. Braly, pp. 151-152.
84. Russell G. Oswald, *Attica: My Story* (Garden City, N.Y: Doubleday, 1972), p. 33.
85. Special Commission on Attica, p. 195.
86. *Ibid.,* p. 53.
87. Sykes, p. 88.
88. Joint Commission on Correctional Manpower and Training, *A Time to Act* (Washington, D.C: Joint Commission on Correctional Manpower and Training, 1969), p. 19.
89. William Cahn, "Report on the Nassau County Jail," *Crime and Delinquency* 19 (January 1973): 10.
90. *Ibid.*
91. Oswald, p. 33.
92. Sykes, pp. 40-62.
93. Cited in Richard A. Cloward, "Social Control in the Prison," in *Prison Within Society: A Reader in Penology,* ed. Lawrence Hazelrigg (Garden City, N.Y: Doubleday, 1969), p. 96.
94. Pell, p. 119.

Chapter Four

Women's Prisons

The types of crimes for which women are convicted include forgery, drug addiction, drug pushing, embezzlement, blackmail, and prostitution. Women also commit crimes of passion such as murder, and impulsive crimes such as shoplifting.[1] While there is no clear indication that women commit fewer crimes than men, it is clear that fewer women are convicted of crimes. Few women spend time in jails and are sent to prison.

Today in the United States only one woman for every eight men is arrested and for every 25 men only one woman is incarcerated in a federal, state, or local prison. Ignoring the local institutions which house only short term prisoners, one finds that out of a prison population of some 400,000 less than 5 percent are female. Unquestionably the criminal justice system treats women more leniently than men for several identifiable reasons: their crimes are not as violent, they pose less of a threat to society than men, and juries are reluctant to send a young girl, a wife, or a mother to jail.[2]

The woman entering prison for the first time faces a severe shock and then a period of painful adjustment. The newly incarcerated woman experiences a variety of feelings — anger, hate, deprivation, anxiety, futility, and loss of identity. Her experiences upon being convicted of a crime and imprisoned are a series of nightmares. Even the removal of the new inmate's personal possessions is an act carrying meaning beyond the simple process of taking away a quantity of commodities. It destroys some of the woman's self-identity or self-image. This removal of personal possessions is a deeply depriving act. A woman's clothes, her jewelry, her shoes, and especially her necessary purse are extensions of her personality. When these items are abruptly confiscated, a part of her is taken away.

The abruptness of this transition is described by Sarah Harris as she relates the experience of four women entering the former New York City

99

House of Detention for Women. When their purses were abruptly taken away during the booking process, one of the women became quite disturbed and began to plead for some of the items in her purse. The matron refused to give her any of the cosmetics in the handbag, her prescription pills, or even her glasses. The prospect of getting along without her glasses was overwhelming to the woman because she could not see anything without them. After some hysteria and a good deal of pleading, the woman was allowed to keep her glasses.[3]

The admission process becomes even more demoralizing for the woman as it proceeds. The procedures of admission into the prison include actions that humiliate, debase, and mortify the newly arrived. Harris, in describing the continuation of the admission procedures, describes the feelings of the four women as they are ordered to strip and shower before being subjected to a rectal search by another inmate. None of the four women had ever experienced such extensive invasions of their privacy.[4]

The woman newly arrived in prison spends time in an orientation section. After being told the rules and regulations of the institution, she is required to make some sort of adjustment to the fact that her freedom is gone and that the prison is to be her home. Separation from her family, her husband or lover, and her children will cause the most pain. But the absence of privacy[5], the lack of a social life, and the complete removal of male companionship intensifies the impact of being locked away. Self-respect begins to disappear. She will be forced to live with women that she may dislike, but her feelings do not matter. For a short period of time, the shock of being in prison probably numbs the impact of prison life. However, unless her sentence is short or in the unlikely event that she can maintain close contact with her family and friends on the outside, the prison will soon become her world.

Incarcerated women adjust to their new lives in different ways. Esther Heffernan, in *Making It in Prison: The Square, The Cool, and The Life*, describes three basic reactions: (1) The square is a noncriminal who, perhaps in a moment of uncontrolled rage, murdered a husband who had been physically and mentally abusive for years. She strives to earn the respect of her sister inmates and officers by focusing on the code of her home town. She wants to be a "good Christian woman." (2) The recidivist prostitute, shoplifter, pusher and/or user of drugs epitomizes the life group, who represent over 50 percent of the inmate population. Prison life becomes important and meaningful to them.[6] To stand firm against prison authority and what it stands for, as the garment workers' local labor organizer speaks out against Butte Knitting Company, is regarded as meritorious. (3) The sophisticated, professional offender—the cool—is from the underground world of organized crime. With aloofness, she dispassionately manipulates her environment, but seldom truly participates in prison life because she is merely visiting for a time.[7] She has prestige, power, and wealth in prison. She "has it all together."

Prison life is not easily dissected. Women, as men, select different patterns of adjustment. Yet regardless of the role the new inmate will play, it rejects her and forgets her. Within a few weeks, the female offender adjusts to her new environment. She learns to accept the prison as home. She will begin to be a part of prison life—to make friends and a new life for herself. At first fearful of the guards and some of the inmates, she begins to slide into her new social world comprised of the sister inmates with whom she lives and works.[8]

PRISON FAMILIES

Organization and Roles

The social organization of correctional institutions where women are placed is centered around a family system. The array of family oriented roles is extensive. It includes father, mother, brothers and sisters, aunts and uncles, and grandmothers and grandchildren.[9] Because of different characteristics, different inmates will play specific roles; for example, the young first offender might be the baby sister in a family unit and elder long-timer could be the grandmother or grandfather. The extent to which the roles are internalized and acted out by each family member is impressive. In the New York House of Detention, one woman called "Granny" had a reputation for having a clean house. Her actions, described in detail by another prisoner clearly explain why this reputation was earned.[10]

> After she removed her furniture she would carry a pail of boiling water, reeking of disinfectant, and go down on her hands and knees with a brush and scrub every inch of the floor, a process similar to scrubbing the sidewalk. Next she would take a new pail of water and the odiferous antiseptic and sterilize her walls, plunge both hands and a big rag in the toilet bowl and scour that, and finally open the corridor windows and vigorously shake the ragged scraps of carpeting that served to cover a few inches of her floor. Every couple of weeks all her flopping shower curtains would be hauled down and others, stiffly starched, would take their place. This type of cleaning gave her a community reputation equivalent to that of a middle-class suburban matron who is active in church groups, entertains well, and is famous for her apple pies.

Not all family members act out their roles with the unquestioned devotion and enthusiasm of Granny, but the roles are played and the members do interact as a family unit. A new inmate most likely will be asked to join a family group and will serve her sentence as a member of a family—a daughter, a sister, or, if she is serving a long term, she may eventually become a family mother or father. Centering most of her prison life activities around the family, she will eat with her family, watch television with them, and sit with them at special functions. If it can be arranged, the family will live together in the same cottage or dormitory, but the family structure is preserved even if the individual members are scattered throughout the institution. Of course, some prison families will be extremely close knit and others loosely structured.[11]

Prison families attempt to act as much like families on the outside as they can under the circumstances, which at best are constraining. In times of stress and crisis, it is the family structure that stands as a bulwark against threats posed by the rigors of prison life. The prison family also serves as the social unit through which the inmates find a relationship with other families and inmates. With the help of the family, the inmate orients to her incarceration, lives through prison marriages and divorces, goes about her daily work and acquires illicit goods and services. Due to their very nature, prison marriages are not lasting, but the structure of the family unit remains as a stable reference point in the social world of the women's prison. The female prisoner, through her participation in the social framework of the family unit, experience relationships that the institution would otherwise not provide.

The daily activities of the family are framed by the family role perceptions that exist in the free society. Prison parents assume that one of the important tasks to be accomplished is the socialization of their siblings. Parents are assumed to be wiser than children and worthy of the children's respect. Children are taught how to live and survive in the prison; they are given advice about romance and marriage prospects; and they are told how to go about getting a parole. Rose Giallombardo provides some examples of this type of advice being given by parents to socialize their children.[12]

> "Keep your nose clean and stay out of trouble. The officers are on one side and the inmates on the other and never the two shall meet. You say to them what you don't care that they know. They've got the keys. They've got a job to do. They lock doors and unlock them. They go home. They don't really care about us as people.". . .
>
> "Don't put your business in the streets. Don't tell all the inmates your business, but act hep. You should be discreet about important matters.". . .
>
> "Sandy comes to me for advice mostly about studs that kite her. She'll get a kite and she'll come to me and ask me, "Pop, should I write?" And I tell her, "Yes if the guy means what he says and isn't jivey." I tell her, it's not right to go whoring around. "Pick one guy and stick to him, but don't go whoring around."

The inmate can share her heartaches, frustrations, anger, sadnesses, and disappointments with the family members. But family members also argue and fight about the same problems that families on the outside quarrel about. For example, a kid brother may be perceived to be lazy and living off the generosity of the other family members. Siblings become jealous of one another. A daughter who misbehaves can humiliate the family.

Of course, a unisexual family cannot reproduce; even so, the family structure is continually changing because inmate-members are paroled and new inmates are accepted into the family. When a key figure like Granny is paroled, everyone pitches in to find a sterling replacement. While unisexual marriages and divorces occur, once the family roles are accepted, they become binding. The free world taboo against incest is observed in the prison family. However, rules and taboos are broken on the inside as they are on the outside. An incestuous relationship may have to be overlooked occasionally.[13] The family roles do sometimes change: a couple who have divorced may assume a brother and sister relationship or an individual who has been playing a female role may switch to a male role.

Economic Organization of the Family

Although female inmates are allowed to spend $15 to $20 a month at the institution commissary for amenities of life, not all prisoners have access to such relatively large sums. Commissary items available for purchase generally include items like cookies, cigarettes, candy, shower caps, curlers, lipstick, face cream, nail polish, and shampoo.[14] In some prisons, inmates are allowed to receive money from the outside for commissary purchases; seldom are offenders allowed to receive packages or gifts other than money except at Christmas. Even at Christmas the types of presents that may be received are carefully specified. Yet poverty is necessarily a relative concept and the standard of living that the prisoners were accustomed to on the outside usually was not very grand. Chances are good that the offenders did not play golf at the Heritage Hill Country Club or engage Jerome of Exclusive Decor to refurbish their dining room and den every two years.

Still, goods and services available through legal channels in the prison are limited, leaving the inmates at least with the feeling that they are poverty-stricken.[15] In women's institutions inmates can steal institutional supplies, go into business for themselves or hustle other girls for commissary goods. Those inmates assigned desirable jobs, perhaps in the warden's office or in the kitchen, can pilfer state goods quite easily and can supply official information. And there usually is a local tradesman or guard that can be bribed to bring in an order, which may include the most recent issue of *True Story*.[16]

Female and male prisoners are equally ingenious in exploiting the prison environment to better their standard of living. Drugs are stolen from the infirmary, food from the kitchen and dining room, and clothing and cleaning fluid from the laundry. As in prisons for men, services are performed and manufacturing takes place. Florrie Fisher recalls the time they "made hooch in the supply closet."[17]

We got the ingredients by stealing what we could, depending on where we worked. The kitchen help got potatoes, the ones in the hospital boosted alcohol, and the table setters got sugar.

Back behind the closet door we could hear it going "glug, glug, glug," and it sounded great. We must have left it just an hour too long, though, for suddenly the whole thing blew up, spewing sour-smelling liquid and pieces of potato all over the walls and ceiling, the mops, brooms and buckets kept in the closet.

Not all prisoners are able to enjoy the benefits of illegal economic goods, other than a stale cookie from the dining room now and then or a nip from a rap buddy's (conversation partner) home brew on New Year's Day. Certain types of inmates are not allowed by the inmate community to participate in the illicit economy regardless of their financial condition. These are the low status inmates—snitchers, inmate cops, and occasional squares. By reason of the fact that these inmates disobey the code, they are pushed away when it is time to share the scarce illegal goods that circulate in the prison.[18] To carry on a flourishing illegal business requires a certain amount of secrecy and the social types of inmate cop, snitchers, and squares cannot be trusted.

The family is the primary economic unit in the female prison. The family unit cooperates in both the stealing and manufacturing of illicit goods and in the consumption of such goods and services. The inmates frequently need commissary products that they have no money to buy and goods and services that cannot be manufactured or stolen without the cooperation of several inmates. The social fabric of the family provides the cooperative spirit and organization needed to procure goods and services. Each family member feels a responsibility to help provide economic benefits for all the other members of the family. A family shares both the legally obtained goods from the prison commissary and the illicit goods obtained through the sub rosa economic system. Family members have an implicit understanding that the members can borrow items of clothing and other objects from one another. Their spirit of generosity in these borrowing activities, of course, varies from time to time and with different individuals. Their behavior in this respect is not unlike the behavior of a family in the free world, wherein teenage sisters alternately argue over and lovingly share one another's clothes and cosmetics.

Punishment by the staff members—such as the removal of commissary privileges for a time—is softened by the family system or the homosexual dyad. If an inmate who is being punished is deprived of almost all economic goods, other inmates in the family group are expected to give her extra food, clothing, or information obtained from the kitchen, garden, or sewing room.[19]

Because of the reciprocal economic relationship that exists among family members, individual family members who play key economic roles in the subculture are of special importance. For example, the "connect" is an inmate who has a good job assignment in the institution which allows her to have access to information and prison supplies. She is in a position to act as middleman and distributor of goods and services.[20] A "booster" is an inmate who is not only especially successful in opportunistic stealing of institution provisions, but also operates an enterprising business.[21] The connect and the booster are able to fulfill important breadwinner roles in the family structure. If a family member has entrepreneurial talent or is placed in a strategic position where she has access to prison information or supplies, the other family members expect her to develop the skills of the connect or booster.

In the "togetherness" of family life, economic activities play an important role. For example. the lore of making alcoholic beverages may be passed along from mother to daughter or from father to son, with favorite recipes being kept as a family secret. Nor does the family neglect to provide technical training in the fine arts of boosting provisions from the prison kitchen or storeroom, although the classes are not exactly like those conducted in the local Allied City Technical School. The following example involves a family situation wherein Granny and Mary Helen, being expert thieves, had assumed the responsibility of instructing a new family member. [22]

> "Now, look at me," Mary-Helen said, coming down the corridor. "Am I walkin' like I always does?" "Yes," the girl answered. "Now I wan' you to look." Mary-Helen reached up under her skirt and pulled out a foot-high can of orange juice from the kitchen. "Now look again," she instructed. She reached up and replaced the can and then lifted her skirts to show it held firmly above her knees. "Now watch." She walked down the corridor, turned and came back, without any indication that she held anything with her legs. "De elevator opirator stop 'bove de flo'," Granny laughed, "an she jest step up like nothin' wrong."

People first learning about homosexual families in women's prisons have varying reactions. The social scientist is apt to say, "Isn't that an interesting phenomenon?" The moral conscience in many is likely to trigger a comment something like, "They ought to be ashamed" or "That's unnatural and ungodly" or "We should clean up women's prisons." Nonetheless, the social structure is advantageous from the viewpoint of the incarcerated women. By building a family structure, the women are making an effort to overcome the fact that their world is comprised only of women; they are attempting to make their society as much like the outside world as possible.

Within the artifical society created, the offenders play roles which are much like the roles they play or want to play on the outside world. The family structure builds a matrix in which an identity that has meaning on the outside is preserved. Even in economic affairs, particularly with the less sophisticated offenders, their past experiences have been primarily in family unit arrangements. The identity so established in the prison setting is not irrelevant to the identity that a woman has on the outside. For rehabilitation goals, this structure has considerable merit because rehabilitation requires that the individual be able to function after leaving the institution.

In considering the reasons for the family type of social organization in women's prisons, there are no clear-cut answers.[23] A number of reasons have been suggested by researchers—all of which are probably partially valid and plausable. Inmates need a form of affection, a way of relating to people: the family is a way of belonging.[24] Certain types of protection and information are needed for survival in the prison and the family can provide those things. Material goods and services beyond those provided by the prison are not absolutely essential, but they are desired. The family is useful in obtaining both legal (from the prison commissary) and illegal goods and services. Another plausible explanation for the type of social structure found in women's prisons is in terms of their preinstitution experiences. The family is the form of social organization that they have been a part of and so is the type that they feel comfortable with.

PRISON LOVE AND MARRIAGE

While the new inmate is being absorbed into a family, she may be experiencing another type of alliance. Experts on the subject do not agree, but most estimates are that between 50 to 70 percent of the inmates in women's prisons in the United States engage in some sort of homosexual activity. Furthermore, David A. Ward and Gene G. Kassebaum point out that even if only 50 percent are engaged in a homosexual alliance, the prison atmosphere is one of homosexual activity.[25] If we accept their statement and consider the range of the estimates on the extent of homosexual activity in women's prisons, it is obvious that homosexuality plays a central role in the daily life of women inmates. The extent of homosexual activity in girls' schools is thought to be even higher—in the vicinity of 70 percent.[26] The basic cause, of course, is the absence of the opportunity for heterosexual activity.[27] In the world of female inmates, the only men around are maintenance crews, ministers and priests, doctors, parole board members, possibly a male warden, and occasionally a husband, boyfriend, or brother vists. For some women, certainly not all, life pivots around her man or men or at least around a romantic relationship. Ward and Kassebaum, in *Women's Prisons,* conclude that the homosexual relationship in female institutions fills this void; it provides an intimate, affectionate relationship with security and social status.[28] Homosexual relationships that develop among female inmates are used to soften the impact of life in the penitentiary. The women strive to develop relationships that strengthen their ability to bear the emotional, social, and economic deprivations of institutional life.[29]

HOMOSEXUAL TYPES

There are basically two types of women who fall into the general category of homosexual. Those women who prefer homosexual activities to heterosexual activities in the free world are called true lesbians. Inmates frequently refer to these women as being sick or perverted. Investigators suspect that a large portion of these dedicated homosexuals are of the social types known as politicians and merchants in men's prisons. Ward and Kassebaum believe that they are like the experienced male convict who is not concerned with doing his time and winning an early release; rather he intends to make prison a way of life by getting a comfortable job and obtaining some material comforts.[30] For this type of female prisoner, prison life has advantages that outweigh the disadvantages.

The other general type that is involved in prison homosexuality is the penitentiary or jailhouse "turnout." This inmate engages in homosexual relations as a way of adjusting to prison life, but in the free world she prefers heterosexual activity. Factors that contribute to her decision to "turnout" include the sheer boredom of living a caged life and the pressure of being sought after by girls who consider her to be attractive. But more often than not a jailhouse turnout will accept a female lover for economic reasons. Harris illustrates how a new inmate learns about the economic advantages involved. The new inmate had noticed that Rusty, a prison butch, always wore nice sweaters. When the new inmate asked Rusty how she managed to obtain such clothes, Rusty introduced her to a girl who worked in the clothing room. Within a few hours, novice Patrica returned to her cell to find a new sweater on her bed. Rusty had introduced the new girl as "good people"—implying that she was to be granted the special favors due to the cooperative.[31]

Should she decide to be half of a homosexual couple, the new inmate will choose to play the role of a man or a woman. If she plays the male role, she will be called a "stud broad," "daddy," "bulldyke," or "butch" and will try to act and look as masculine as possible. If she chooses to play the female role, she will be tagged as a "femme" or "mommy" and be courted by a stud broad.

Butches

"Drag butches," trying to be as manly as possible, cut their hair in a male fashion. They attempt to walk and sit like men. They even make an effort to hold and puff on cigarettes as men do. If institutional regulations allow it, they would prefer to wear slacks, ties, and shirts cut in a mannish style. Sometimes they will wear neckerchiefs as ties. At events where dresses or skirts are required, innumerable disguises are used to hide their feminine attire.[32] Butches prefer men's shorts and tee shirts, which can be easily made in the sewing department, to bras, girdles, and panties.

Not all stud broads dress in drag (men's clothes) or attempt to look and act like a man. Some sophisticated butches feel that such behavior is merely a facade—that clothes do not "make the man." Butches display the courtesies that men perform for women, such as opening doors, lighting cigarettes, and getting the refreshments. They play the aggressive role in the courtship and marriage relationships and act as the spokesman for the couple.

Researchers have attempted to determine if those prisoners who play the role of the butch are markedly different from prisoners who play the role of a femme, or those who do not participate in homosexual activities at all. The evidence is inconclusive; nonetheless, authorities do indicate that butches tend to be more homely than the general run of female prisoners. A young woman who is rather plain and dowdy may be told outright by a seasoned con that she would make a good butch—thus defining for her the role that she can play in the prison community. Yet there is no physiological characteristic that is statistically significantly different from that of the other prisoners. In a study done by Ward and Kassebaum, the butches had had less heterosexual experience than others before being imprisoned. In short, many of them have been less involved with men. Undoubtedly, butches are reacting to a number of factors both within and outside the prison.[33]

Economic need is a potential cause for becoming a butch. In the county jail, an old con might say, "Wow, if you don't have any money coming in, cut your hair and drop your belt and wear high socks and you've got it made,' and that's right. They do that and they come in—they've got all kinds of girls chasing them, buying them coffee, cigarettes, knitting them sweaters, and you name it, they've got it."[34] Prestige seems to be associated with playing the male role.[35] Once in a while a butch chooses to shift from the male to the female role, called "dropping the belt." This frowned upon act causes a loss of status to the one shifting. Since "on the reservation" there is a preponderance of femmes over butches, "dropping the belt" intensifies this supply shortage. Femmes may shift to the butch role, but that is not customary either.

Femmes

For a femme, physical attractiveness has much to do with her popularity. It is said that models, dancers, or strippers are in great demand. A high-priced call girl commands considerable respect. The younger the woman, the more desirable. Although femmes are of higher status than those women who do not participate in homosexual relationships, they are of lesser status than butches.[36] There are exceptions in this type of prestige ranking—a few infamous inmates, notorious because of their exploits and impressive criminal records in organized crime, receive high status because of their reputation as well as their wealth and power.

The femme plays the stereotyped role of the woman: that is to say, she is submissive and does the housekeeping. She does the cleaning, the sewing, the bed making, and frequently the commissary shopping. She performs the functions of a nonliberated housewife. Should a femme be penniless, the stud broad will become a "commissary hustler" to provide goods for the wife if she is particularly fond of her.

COURTSHIP

A valuable source of information about the "going together" or courtship relationship between two inmates is their clandestine kites (letters) to each other. Most reformatories and prisons forbid the exchanging of notes—an official policy that does not appear to dampen enthusiasm for this activity. Possibly it adds the dimension of fear and excitement because the writer is in danger of getting caught. In this respect, two important research studies have been conducted, both describing the youthful female offender; the first, by Sidney Kosofsky and Albert Ellis, involved the analysis of 100 notes, randomly selected from several hundred illegal letters confiscated by the officers in a reformatory for female juvenile delinquents[37]; and the latest research by A.J.W. Taylor, which consists of a careful study of 46 notes passed between close friends in a New Zealand reformatory for girls.[38] Kosofsky and Ellis reported that the notes were written on all sorts of scrounged paper, ranging from pages torn from books or magazines to bits and pieces of wrapping paper. Often they were folded into small triangular shapes—thus accounting for the term "kites"—so they could be tucked into a hiding place like a bra or shoe or cover of a book. Kites are passed between girls as they brush past one another going to and from the dining hall, their cottage or work. Sometimes a messenger will be used as an intermediary or the note will be hidden in a dead letter drop (a secret place where it can be recovered later).

The opening and closing sentences quoted from one of the notes confiscated by the researchers is an example of a young girl carefully using lines found in a novel or magazine article as her own: "While sitting here in the deepest of meditation, I thought I would take the greatest of pleasure in dropping you a few lines of love and devotion."[39] Because of their insecurity about themselves, their feelings, and their ability to write appropriate prose, the girls may copy the words of writers who they believe have said the proper and accepted things.[40] Often the notes were embellished with kiss signs (X marks) and other drawings, including pictures cut from magazines. Most of the notes were love letters dealing with the hundreds of intimacies that an infatuated couple share. Like those that pass between adolescent boys and girls, the love letters were less sexual than romantic.[41] The girls, with painstaking care (demonstrated by the many visible erasure marks often found on notes), compose and write down their feelings. A passage from one of these kites found in a library book, which serves as a common hiding place, demonstrates the emotional fervor often felt for each other by the young offenders:[42]

My darling sweetheart!
     Why don't you look at me no more? Why dont you smile at me
no more? I cant sleep nights thinking maybe you dont love me no
more please write me and dont tell me you love nobody else. Id
die if you did. write the way you used to. say you love just me
and if you dont Ill do something awful and youll feel bad. I dont
love nobody but you.

The innocence depicted by the youthful is not necessarily present
among the older female inmates. The femme/stud broad relationship character-
istically seen in prisons for women probably has a less romantic and more
sexual aura. With the passage of time, some of the romantic dreams of a
teenager are gradually replaced by the realities of life. The orientation changes
as the inmate gathers experience on the outside and the inside. The correspondence of women expresses threats, love, jealousy or even anger due to unfaith-
fulness. The following excerpt from an example of a kite in Ward and
Kassebaum's *Women's Prison* illustrates that the tone of the notes between
adult female prisoners can be quite different from that of the youthful
offender.[43]

"My darling and My Secret Love, I miss you so much (no shit).
Hey, like today is my day off plus no school this afternoon and
where are we. Remember when we were talking about our periods
I told you, oh, oh! That's bad. But I never said why. Well, I guess
I am a little bit coo coo (smile). Superstitious maybe but it's
strange how everything I believe in comes true. Yogi (smile) no,
but at first our periods weren't together—but as soon as we start
fucking and doing everything together, we did that too."

Love and Economics
The femme-stud broad relationship is reinforced if not motivated
by economics. A femme often enters into a love relationship because the
butch supplies the items she cannot get in any other way or, at least, the
relationship offers a viable alternative source of goods. In some cases commissary goods (candy, cigarettes, and so on) may be used to entice a femme to
go with the stud broad or, once in awhile, the other way around. The new
femme may be asked for a date, perhaps to go with a butch's crowd.[44] The
nuances of this relationship bears closer inspection.
     In the previous example where the new inmate learned how to
obtain a sweater, the economic and sexual implications were clear.[45] Patricia
experienced a series of frustrations in attempting to get items needed in the
daily life of the prison. In each case, she was frustrated in her attempts to
obtain the items through legitimate means. After obtaining the sweater with
the help of her friend, Rusty, Patricia attempted to obtain bleach for doing

her laundry. She knew that bleach was available within the institution because she smelled it when other inmates were doing their laundry. But when she tried to obtain bleach through legitimate channels, both staff members and inmates expressed surprise and denied that it was available.[46] She had the same type of disappointment when she attempted to obtain a douche bag. Patricia was never able to get either item via legal means, but influential butch Rusty had no difficulty in obtaining the necessary items for her in the illicit sub rosa system. Under such aggravating circumstances, Patricia quickly sensed that she needed a provider to survive in the prison setting.[47]

The economic dimensions of courting and sex and clearly demonstrated in a quotation in Ward and Kassebaum's *Women's Prison*. The initial part of an interesting prison game is illustrated. The inmate being quoted is telling the interviewer about some of her prison experiences, as follows:[48]

> " They were all sort of trying to see who could get to me first. They gave me pajamas, and stuff to drink, they gave me pills to get loaded, weed and smokes and I had an offer for some *stuff* [herion] that I used to use, but I don't anymore so I turned that down. But I took all the stuff [subject is not referring to heroin here] you know—I took it because I needed it, because I don't have anything . . . and I couldn't see those state nightgowns, so I took it, but I never gave anything in return. Some of the girls are pretty salty about it. The only time I did anything—I needed a sweater real bad. This is terrible, it sounds horrible, but I didn't have anything when I came in, they took everything away from me. And I needed a sweater—I was freezing to death. So this one girl I was with in county jail told me, 'Take me to bed and satisfy me and I'll give you a sweater.' And she had a wardrobe that was tremendous, even in here, because she'd been here since year one—she's one of the bigwigs. She's good to know anyway, so I took her to bed and I got my sweater. But I could never do anything like that again, I was loaded when I did it because I couldn't stand it—but I had to have something to wear.

Butches give presents when they are rushing new femmes; but once the devotion and affection of the femme is secure, the butch turns around and demands goods and services from the femmes in exchange for the butch's affirmation of fidelity—that she will not fool around with other femmes.[49] A butch, nonetheless, may demand commissary goods and cigarettes from several femmes at one time.[50] A butch exploits femmes for several reasons, one of which is squarely based on economic motivation. But butches want goods as status symbols as well as for consumption. As symbols of prestige, gifts show that they are beloved by their girls and are in command of the relationship.[51] Such provisions of goods on the part of the femmes is a form of tribute, which demonstrates their loyalty to the butch. The butch, or true lesbian for lack of a better term, does not like or trust the sometime lesbian or jailhouse turnout, knowing that she will revert to heterosexual activity as soon as she leaves prison and returns to a bisexual society. Thus a butch may economically exploit the femme—using her but not trusting her.[52]

MARRIAGE

Within a short period of time after entering the prison, a new femme will usually marry a butch. The marriage relationship will be recognized by other inmates and the two will be referred to as a married couple. Acting as man and wife, they will do everything married couples do given the constraints placed upon them by nature and the need to avoid being caught and punished by the staff. Although the term has several meanings, the couple are said to be "making it." Ordinarily there is an element of romance in the marriage. A ceremony may be performed by Grandma or Daddy with the proper words as, "Do you take this woman?" or "Do you take this man?" Wedding rings may be exchanged and returned to a safe hiding place after the marriage ceremony.

Couples may walk arm in arm in halls and sit close together and hold hands in the movie or while watching television in the recreation room. Needless to say, opportunities for more serious expressions of affection are limited. In the prisons where the women live in cottage housing arrangements, the institution rules often forbid an inmate to close her door when she has a visitor in the room. Still the women can be alone in a room if they employ a pinner (lookout) to watch for staff members. Otherwise, lovers have some limited opportunities to be together during recreation, while in classes, and when moving from one part of the institution to another. The chapel is a favorite spot to rendezvous.

The fleeting moments that couples have to share is described rather pathetically by Helen Bryan in *Inside*. The inmates were returning from the school building at Alderson after listening to Christmas music on records: "I was among the last to leave and as I walked down the steps, heavily shadowed by the pine trees and bushes on either side, I was surprised to bump into couples locked in each others arms."[53] Continuing, Bryan says, "But the embraces could not last long, for in another moment the officers would be coming down the hill. Furthermore, we were required to leave from and return to the cottage in a group, and girls not interested in amorous demonstrations would not wait too long for those who were." She concludes with this detail: "These girls would slowly walk on ahead and the girls involved would have to break away and run to catch up so that all would enter the cottage at the same time."[54]

Prison marriages are not without ups and downs: in other words, they are not all made in heaven. Most fights in women's institutions are rooted in a homosexual triangle. Problems caused by rivals, mistresses, and infidelity sometimes trigger stormy emotions that lead to physical violence complete with the use of weapons such as razor blades and scissors. The women rightfully fear that their faces will be permanently scarred or made ugly.[55] While an inmate at Bedford, Florrie Fisher taught the youthful offenders at Westfield located on the same campus. In pointing out how tough even a school for minor offenders is, she says:[56]

When a mommy and a daddy had a fight at Westfield, the
bull-dyker would stick a scissors in the girl's back, twist it and pull
it out, then dare her to go to the clinic to have it treated. There
were always deaths from blood poisoning or loss of blood because
the kids who got stabbed with scissors or knives were afraid to tell
the guards or go to the clinic. They knew they'd be killed when
they got back.

Prison marriages last for about one year, sometimes a shorter or longer length of time. They obviously must end when the husband or wife is paroled and frequently end before this time because the butch finds herself a more desirable femme. A femme may obtain a more attractive husband, but this is an infrequent event because femmes are more plentiful than stud broads. If one of the parties to a marriage agreement is paroled and the other member is not, the usual conditions of parole will prohibit them from seeing one another. A woman newly released from prison has problems more pressing than seeing her old prison friends. But more to the point, the women want to begin new lives or go back to their old ones—to put aside the unpleasant memories of confinement.[57]

Economics of Marriage

As previously noted, the femme in the marriage arrangement does the housework, laundry, commissary buying, and other assorted wifely chores. The butch may play the role of commissary hustler if the wife is poverty-stricken and they have a "good" relationship.[58] Some stud broads have an arrangement with several femmes solely to use them. The femme who is a victim of this exploitation is called a "trick." A commissary hustler may marry a femme living in her cottage and also establish relationships with a number of other femmes located in different cottages in the institution. The arrangement is known as "mating for commissary reasons."[59] The commissary hustler will send a commissary list to each of her tricks scattered throughout the prison and the tricks are supposed to fill the list.

The explanation for this relationship is solely economic in that the trick is a source of income for the butch.[60] Rusty, the super butch in *Hellhole*, acknowledges her economic motivation while philosophizing about her hustling. She notes that playing with three or four femmes, each of whom has about seven dollars to spend each month, can be lucrative. The femmes are able to buy a lot of cigarettes for their butch. In turn, the cigarettes can buy a number of favors from girls who do not have any income.[61]

The trick will allow herself to be exploited because she knows no other way to survive and because she is hopeful that the butch will change her romantic inclinations and become genuinely fond of her.[62] Heffernan interestingly comments that "breadwinning" is part of the man's role in the middle-class,[63] but not in the lower socioeconomic class to which most of the inmates belong. She also may be afraid of her butch. Commissary hustlers are regarded as exploiters by inmates. One penologist notes that the inmates feel that the commissary hustler is the type of woman who would exploit men on the outside, but she must turn her exploitation to women because no men are available.[64]

The commissary hustler's organization resembles the organization of a pander with his prostitutes or, in the street vernacular, a pimp and his stable. The similarity in these two illegal business organizations, one inside the walls and the other outside, was recognized by a nineteen-year-old prostitute named Mary Thomas. After she had completed her jail sentence and gone back to her former male pimp, she remarked that Big Time Reed, her prison butch, came to behave like a male pimp once their relationship was firmly established. The butch soon began to prevail upon Mary to buy her items at the commissary and to do her laundry as well as keep her cell clean.[65]

SUMMARY OF LOVE, MARRIAGE, AND FAMILY

The subculture that the new inmate quickly becomes a part of centers on the family unit comprised of mother, father, sisters, brothers, aunts, uncles, grandparents—a complete family unit that imitates the family found on the outside. In all likelihood the new inmate will be asked to join a family unit, which will become a protecting social and economic cocoon during her sentence in prison. The specific role in the family that she will assume depends on her background, her appearance, her age, and her preference. Her choice of whether to play the role of a man or a woman will also be important should the inmate decide to court and participate in marriage — the most volatile of the prison relationships. The economic system that inmates take part in and operate, although partially a formal system in that it involves commissary goods purchased from the state-operated store, is heavily oriented to illicit use of stolen or manufactured goods. Here again, it is in the family and the butch/femme relationships that the basic sub rosa entrepreneurial units are found. Women in prison try to reproduce in bits and pieces the socioeconomic systems with which they were familiar on the outside.

SPECIAL ROLES

Around, within, and through the family, courting and marriage relationships and other roles are acted out. It is necessary to examine these roles in order to get a complete picture of how the female subculture operates socially, politically, and economically, and to understand at least cursorily the dimensions of the life of the female offender. Some of the argot roles were obviously differentiated because of the economic function involved. Of course, once the economic designation has been established, it almost immediately begins to carry sociopolitical overtones.[66] First we will examine the roles of the booster and the connect, who, with the commissary hustler, are the entrepreneurs of the sub rosa economy. Then the role of the "homey," who is bought off with economic goods, will be described. The outlaws of the system—malicious snitchers and the inmate cops—are discussed at the conclusion of this chapter.

Boosters and Connects

Inmates make a clear distinction between a woman who occasionally pilfers an item for her own consumption and the booster. Almost all inmates steal small amounts of food, such as coffee and sugar from the dining room and kitchen. These inmates are not in business. It is said that even the inmate cops and squares will steal from the state to brighten up a dull Sunday afternoon. The booster, sometimes called a "merchant" or "politician," is a different breed; she owns and manages a business and is recognized as an entrepreneur by other inmates.[67] She steals only from state sources—never from her sister inmates—and steals in volume sufficient to sell to other inmates. Whereas the cools, often having had experience in the complex economic world of organized crime, could bring sophisticated managerial skills to prison businesses, they seldom do. Hustling in women's prisons belongs to the small-time operator.[68] Fisher, in *The Lonely Trip Back*, describes how as a booster she earned the cash to support her drug habit while in prison.[69]

> I solved this by building up a tidy business selling triple-decker sandwiches to the girls with ready money. A triple-decker was roast beef on one slice, bologna on the second slice, and jelly or peanut butter on the third. A very tasty sandwich.
> I'd steal the bread and the makings in the kitchen, and boost them out between my legs. I could boost anything, a can of juice, a jar of pickles, half the sliced bologna in the refrigerator. It became more and more of a challenge to see just how big a load I could walk out with, neatly hidden under my skirt.[69]

Boosters also perform valued services for inmates as well as selling materials or equipment they had stolen from state sources. Virginia McManus vividly

vividly describes another booster's activities in the following testimony, taken from *Not For Love*. Two new inmates, incarcerated on a prostitution charge, are returning to their cell from the clothing room where they have just received their issue of clothing.[70]

> Bea said, "You know, except for the old women I don't see anybody in dresses like these." She was right—almost everyone wore solid-color dresses, made in straight sack-dress style, very tight, pegged at the bottom and stiff with starch. Our dresses were limp as dust rags.
>
> "You come on in my house after lunch," Barbara said, "and I'll get your clothes fixed up."
>
> In Barbara's cell there were stacks of solid-colored dresses, pins, needles, thread and, under the mattress, scissors. "You've just got to have connections," she said, pinning one to my size. "It's just like in the streets, you've got to have connections. Now, it'll cost you a pack of cigarettes for each dress they make fit you down in the sewing room, and a pack every time you want one washed and starched."

More often than not an influential booster is a butch and also operates as a commissary hustler. A booster has learned to use her environment, to get on in a world which she regards as tough. She may believe that hustling is easier inside than outside the institution, and for her it may be. On the inside she has everything she wants—clothes, food, cigarettes, pills, and women. Boosters may fight for territorial rights. For example, a stud broad returning to her prison home may fight to reclaim her old territory, clients, and markets. This is an infrequent occurrence, however, for generally there is plenty of business for everyone—so much that boosters will sometimes help one another.

A striking contrast between the male and female prison cultures is the difference in acceptance of the merchant role. While the term merchant denotes low status in the male prison culture, the activities of the booster (as female counterpart of the merchant) are admired and bring her honor.[71] The other inmates admire the booster for engaging in successful business activities. She is respected the same way a woman who sells Avon products on the outside is respected—"She is just trying to help out the family." They may comment to the effect that, "If you can get a little racket going, more power to you."[72] The economic activities of the prestigious male inmate leader are also accepted by the male inmate. It is the role of commissary hustler that involves the payment of a commission by the femmes that the female inmates loathe.

The connect is distinguished from the booster in the prison argot. A connect has a choice assignment in the warden's office, infirmary or kitchen, a place where knowledge about prison activities can be acquired and a place where scarce goods can be stolen. The connects perform the functions of middlemen: they steal, store, and distribute goods and pass on prison gossip.[73] While the booster demonstrates some talent as an enterpriser, the connect's good fortune is more often than not due to an opportune job assignment.

Homey

A "homey" is the designation given to an inmate who is from another inmate's hometown or region. Homies usually have not known each other on the outside, but while in prison a relationship is thrust upon them. When a new inmate arrives at the prison, her dossier, including her home town, is circulated throughout the institution as surely as if it had been broadcast on the six o'clock evening news. A homey immediately tends to the needs of the new arrival. Cigarettes, soap, toothbrush, toiletries, required commissary items are supplied to the new homey. In effect, homies have a form of mutual aid society; they have the right to turn to one another in time of need. The supplies provided represent a loan, to be repaid at a later date. The motivation of a homey can be clearly understood as an investment that will pay dividends in the future. Through economic cooperation, the homies attempt to form an alliance that will insure that neither will gossip about the other after leaving the prison and going back home.[74]

Snitchers

A study at Frontera Prison, apparently one that gave rather imprecise results, estimated that between 50 to 90 percent of the inmates "snitched"—that is, gave information to the officials when a sister inmate disobeyed the rules in one way or another.[75] Some researchers have suggested that women's prisons are a society of snitchers. There is a feeling among inmates that "women are women," and "you know women."[76] These sentiments express the vague belief that almost all women have this defect and they ought to be accepted as being defective in this way. From a woman's liberationist point of view, such an attitude is an insidious result of a male chauvinist system. Ward and Kassebaum provide insight into the feelings of an old-timer toward snitching. At the time of the interview she was under the pressure of a staff investigation into the theft of some demerol from the hospital.[77]

> "You can't put pressure on squealers—a few of us would like
> to—because this would be reported right away. The only people
> who don't snitch are a few old-time inmates, especially those from
> Tehachapi (the location of the prison prior to 1952). If you could
> just get the inmates not to cop out on everything—even if they

did when it meant more time for them or someone was to get
hurt—this would be an improvement. As far as I'm concerned,
however, there are no times when I'd cop out."

However, there are varying degrees of snitching. Women inmates
accept the fact that most of the girls will snitch to officials when it serves
their purpose to do so, when they are revengeful, or angry or jealous because
a butch is fickle or when stolen goods are not being shared in the way an
inmate feels they should be.[78] Under these circumstances inmates shrug their
shoulders and say "girls will be girls."

There are two other types of snitchers that are not so readily
accepted: the "stool pigeon" and the "jive bitch." The jive bitch, a troublemaker and a liar, is never trusted by inmates and undoubtedly should not be
regarded as trustworthy by the staff of the prison.[79] She spreads lies and
gossip about families and couples to the staff and other inmates merely to
create disharmony and trouble. The stool pigeon, despised by her sister
inmates, is a pawn of the prison officers and systematically provides the
officers with information. Often the officials will shift the stoolie from place
to place in the prison. Both inmates and officers who negotiate with stoolies
loathe them. Violent treatment of the stoolie is not unknown, but inmates
customarily choose to handle a professional stoolie without violence. Instead
of brute force, the inmates use processes called "panning" and "signifying."
These processes involve discussing the inmate in a particularly unpleasant way
or mimicking her either when she is present or in her absence.[80] Some penologists maintain that the inmates condemn the professional snitcher, not on
ethical grounds but for the practical reason that their activities break up the
solidarity of the inmate community and destroys the ability of the inmates to
carry out their sub rosa activities. The presence of a large number of snitchers
certainly severely limits the operations of the illicit economic system and the
progress of love affairs. These female social types are comparable to the rats,
center men, and weakling roles found in the male prison.

Sometimes a woman is coded as a criminal, not because of a
background of slum living, deprivation, and prostitution, but because she,
inadvertently or by choice, became involved with a man who asked her to
drive the "getaway" car or pass the forged check—she is a criminal almost
by accident, she is a square. A square brings to prison her middleclass beliefs,
values, and orientation. The inmate culture is alien to her way of life and her
thinking patterns. The other inmates know that the innocence and naïvete of
the square is potentially dangerous because she is oriented to the staff
values.[81] For example, an innocent comment about a fellow prisoner's new
sweater could cause that inmate to serve days in solitary confinement. Squares
are not hated, but rather simply avoided. Here, as in other situations, the
inmates often show clear insight regarding their sisters. The square is naive;
that is why she is in prison.

Inmate Cops

Some prisoners play the role of an "inmate cop" who is placed by the prison officials in a position of having at least limited authority over her sister inmates. This occurs in the context of a supervisory work assignment or a clerk's position involving the issuing of orders or reporting of illegal activities. Penologists report that this role is resented severely by prisoners, who dislike the breaking up of their supposed solidarity and who tend to feel that the officers should run their own prison. Yet in female penitentiaries there is less importance attached to inmate loyalty and the group code, with the "right guy" type of behavior being much less the ideal of the group.[82] The inmate cop identifies with the staff, acting and believing as staff members do. In reality she probably thinks of herself as part of the staff and, therefore, does not perceive of herself as breaking any code because she is not breaking hers.

SUMMARY

This chapter has summarized the framework of economic activity in the female inmate culture. Most of the research in female institutions indicates that the family structure is the dominant mode of social organization within that setting. The butch/femme courting and marriage relationship, being rather unstable, functions within the overall family structure. Much of the illicit economic activity in women's prisons takes place within the family unit. The family is an economic unit that produces, consumes, and shares. Boosters, who are the merchants of the female prisons, may be a part of an extended family unit and share and provide for it, or they may be commissary hustlers with a setup that resembles the arrangement that a madam has with her prostitutes or a procurer (pimp) has with his staff.

After reviewing the economic behavior of women in prison, we have come to the conclusion that the illegal economic organizations they develop are not at all unique or surprising. Women in prison are generally from low middle and low socioeconomic backgrounds. Women from these strata of society are more oriented to their men, their homes, and their children. When they have been gainfully employed outside the home they have been in occupations that clearly were an extension of the jobs they performed as lovers, wives, and mothers. In addition, for a woman to help out with a small sandwich business or to take in laundry is admirable. So the booster is admired in prison. With the butch/femme relationship, where the butch initially courts with gifts and later demands tribute, often from a number of women at the same time, you see the same organization that pimps have successfully used for years, except in this case the enterprising and merchandising role is played by a woman who is regarded as a man.

In comparing the female prison culture with the male culture, a number of important questions are raised. To what extent is the social organization different? What do the differences imply for operation of the sub rosa economic system? What accounts for the differences in the two systems? These questions are addressed in the next chapter.

Notes to Chapter 4

1. James V. Bennet, *I Chose Prison* (New York: Alfred A. Knopf, 1970), pp. 127-141 and Rose Giallombardo, *Society of Women: A Study of a Women:s Prison* (New York: John Wiley, 1966), p. 89

2. Bennett, p. 129.

3. Sara Harris, *Hellhole* (New York: E. P. Dutton, 1967), pp. 25-26.

4. *Ibid.*, p. 26.

5. Creighton Brown Burnham, *Born Innocent* (Englewood Cliffs, N.J.: Prentice-Hall, 1958), pp. 92-93.

6. Esther Heffernan, *Making It in Prison: The Square, The Cool, and The Life,* (New York: John Wiley, 1972), pp. 41 and 145.

7. *Ibid.*, pp. 146 and 158-159.

8. Joanna Kelley, *When the Gates Shut* (London: Longmans, Green, 1967), p. 31.

9. Bennet, pp. 138-139.

10. Virginia McManus, *Not For Love* (New York: G. P. Putnam's Sons, 1960), p. 227.

11. Giallombardo, pp. 165-189.

12. *Ibid.*, pp. 166-167.

13. *Ibid.*, pp. 172-173.

14. *Ibid.*, pp. 119-120.

15. F. E. Haynes, "The Sociological Study of the Prison Community," *The Journal of Criminal Law and Criminology* 39 (November-December 1948): 439, and Giallombardo, p. 97.

16. Burnham, pp. 112-113.

17. Florrie Fisher, *The Lonely Trip Back* (Garden City, N.Y.: Doubleday, 1971), p. 145.

18. Giallombardo, pp. 106-117.

19. Giallombardo, p. 121.

20. Giallombardo, p. 120.

21. *Ibid.*, pp. 120-121.

22. McManus, p. 235.

23. John H. Gagnon and William Simon, "The Social Meaning of Prison Homosexuality," *Federal Probation 32 (March 1968): 28.*

24. Rose Giallombardo, "Social Roles in a Prison for Women," *Social Problems 13* (Winter 1966): 271-272.

25. David A. Ward and Gene G. Kassebaum, *Women's Prisons: Sex and Social Structure* (Chicago: Aldine, 1965), pp. 92-93.

26. Seymour L. Halleck and Marvin Hersko. "Homosexual Behavior in A Correctional Institution for Adolescent Girls," *American Journal of Orthopsychiatry* 32 (October 1962): 913.

27. Gagnon and Simon, 28.

28. Ward and Kassebaum, p. 76.

29. A. J. W. Taylor, "The Significance of 'Darls' or 'Special Relationships' for Borstal Girls," *The British Journal of Criminology* 5 (October 1965): 417.

30. Ward and Kassebaum, p. 118.

31. Harris, p. 230.

32. McManus, p. 237.

33. Ward and Kassebaum, pp. 110-113.

34. *Ibid.*, p. 144.

35. Giallombardo, *Society of Women*, p. 124.

36. Harris, pp. 232-234.

37. Sidney Kosofsky and Albert Ellis, "Illegal Communication Among Institutionalized Female Delinquents," *The Journal of Social Psychology* 48 (August 1958): 155-160.

38. Taylor, 406-418.

39. Kosofsky and Ellis, 156.

40. *Ibid.*, 159.

41. Taylor, 411.

42. Helen Bryan, *Inside* (Boston: Houghton Mifflin, 1953), pp. 279-280.

43. Ward and Kassebaum, p. 157.

44. *Ibid.*, p. 145.

45. Haris, p. 230.

46. *Ibid.*

47. *Ibid.*, pp. 230-232.

48. Ward and Kassebaum, p. 148.

49. *Ibid.*, p. 178.

50. Harris, pp. 232-234.

51. Ward and Kassebaum, p. 192.

52. Harris, p. 235.

53. Bryan, p. 281.

54. *Ibid.*

55. Giallombardo, "Social Roles," 274.

56. Fisher, p. 145.

57. Bryan, p. 277.

58. Giallombardo, *Society of Women*, p. 150.

59. *Ibid.*, p. 125.

60. Harris, pp. 232-234.

61. *Ibid.*, p. 235.

62. Giallombardo, *Society of Women*, pp. 125-126.

63. Heffernan, p. 96.

64. Giallombardo, *Society of Women*, p. 126.

65. Harris, p. 240.

66. Giallombardo, "Social Role," 285 and McManus, pp. 234-235.

67. Heffernan, p. 79.

68. *Ibid.*, p. 168.

69. Fisher, p. 97.

70. McManus, pp. 221-222.

71. Giallombardo, "Social Roles," 280.

72. Giallombardo, *Society of Women*, p. 121.

73. *Ibid.*, p. 120.

74. *Ibid.*, pp. 118-119.

75. Ward and Kassebaum, p. 33.

76. Giallombardo, "Social Roles," 285.

77. Ward and Kassebaum, p. 33.

78. Giallombardo, *Society of Women*, p. 107.

79. Bennett, pp. 138-139.

80. Giallombardo, *Society of Women,* p. 110.
81. Giallombardo, "Social Roles," 277.
82. Ward and Kassebaum, p. 53.

Chapter Five

Differences in Prison Cultures of Men and Women

DIFFERENCES IN CORRECTIONAL' LITERATURE

The two preceding chapters indicated that the social organization of male prisons and that of female prisons differs substantially. Virtually all researchers who have studied the informal social organization in either men's or the women's prisons agree that the differences are significant. However, there is not complete agreement as to the reasons for the differences. Nonetheless, there is noteworthy speculation in the correctional literature concerning the causes of the differences; it will be profitable to review some of these hypotheses before addressing the issue of how the different social structures affect the sub rosa economic transactions.

The studies of both female and male prison cultures posit that the adoption of specific roles within the prison culture is the result of the inmates's reaction to the pain and suffering resulting from his incarceration—that imprisonment causes severe deprivation and the inmate must find some means of adjusting to the deprivation to ease the pain as much as possible. Thus the argot term "making it," as used in female institutions, implies that the inmate must make concessions and changes in her usual life style in order to adjust to prison life and make it as painless as possible. Failing to make special adjustments results in doing "hard time," an argot term familiar to both male and female prisoners. From their use of special language, it would appear that inmates agree with the sociologists in thinking that inmate modes of adjustment to prison life—the way they organize, share economic goods, and regard officials—are caused by the deprivations of incarceration.

Ward and Kassebaum and Motherhood

David A. Ward and Gene G. Kassebaum follow the same train of
thought in their *Women's Prison: Sex and Social Structure.* They, too, make
careful note of the nature of deprivations borne in the prison environment
and attempt to distinguish between the kinds of losses experienced by female
prisoners as opposed to those suffered by male inmates. Ward and Kassebaum
use the basic list of deprivations noted by Gresham M. Sykes for male
prisons[1] and add one type of suffering that they feel is unique to female
prisoners; that is, they argue that women undergo exactly the same types of
suffering that men experience plus one more, which is related to their sex
role.

Ward and Kassebaum note that the biological fact of femininity,
coupled with the traditional division of labor between men and women with
respect to the rearing of small children, gives the female a special "mother
role." The additional anguish experienced by the event which they term
"dispossession of the mother role" causes acute pain to the female prisoner—a
form of pain not felt by the male inmate.[2] In support of their position, they
offer the information that their research subjects at Frontera were largely a
group of women who had direct experience in the mother role. Sixty-eight
percent of the prisoners there were mothers, and 59 percent were the mothers
of minor children.[3] They conclude that the role dispossession creates acute
frustration and their research also indicates that the frustration does not lessen
over time.[4] In assessing the reaction of women prisoners to the special pains
of imprisonment, Ward and Kassebaum express their belief that the special
family social structure of female prisons arises because the women continue in
roles similar to those which they knew in their preinstitution condition.

Giallombardo and Women's Role

Rose Giallombardo's investigations of the informal social structure
of the Federal Reformatory for Women at Alderson, West Virginia, were
conducted independently but at roughly the same time as the Ward and
Kassebaum research. Her separate conclusions concerning the cause of the
major differences between the social structures of male and female prisons are
similar to the conclusions of Ward and Kassebaum. Giallombardo concludes
that the female inmate's behavior can only be understood within the matrix
of her social role as a woman, her psychological differences, and her social
position. Since Giallombardo formed her conclusions in the early and mid
1960s, they precede the full impact of the Women's Liberation movement—
this fact is obvious to any reader of her work. But to ignore her work would
be unwise, for her findings are based on the study of a group of inmates who
do not come from the world of the liberated women. Most women prisoners
are drawn from the lower socioeconomic classes as opposed to the middle and
upper socioeconomic classes, where the feminist movement has flowered.

Giallombardo maintains that women have established roles to play. Outside the prison they are daughters, sisters, wives, and mothers within a basic family unit wherein the man is responsible for economic security and the woman is the homemaker. Even if the mother works, child rearing remains a part of her primary responsibility; she must place the welfare of her children and management of her home first and the demands of her occupation second: her life is to be centered on marriage and child rearing. In a male-dominated society such as ours, the man is supposed to establish the family unit by choosing a helpmate. An aspiring young woman will dutifully try to be sexually attractive in order to be selected by a male and to begin to fulfill her ordained roles as wife and mother within the family unit. She is taught to be unobtrusive and subtle, while her mate learns to be aggressive. However, the woman also learns to manipulate males to achieve her goals in life.[5] If her home is abundantly happy, her marriage apparently successful and secure, and her children do not misbehave, she is an acceptable human being in the eyes of God and mankind.

Giallombardo believes that women are socialized so that their motivations tend to be emotional and that they derive their main satisfactions from love, affection, and service to their families.[6] Because of the different socialization received by women, Giallombardo concludes that women make adjustments to prison which are fundamentally different from the adjustments made by males: "Kinship and marriage ties make it possible for the inmates to ascribe and achieve social statuses and personalities in the prison other than that of inmate which are consistent with the cultural expectations of the female role in American society."[7]

Summary of Comparisons

Most of the comparisons of the male and female prison cultures have been done by reasearchers concerned primarily with women's prisons. Sociological research, as is other types, is somewhat faddish and trendy: one finds a body of literature concentrating on the male prison subculture clustered around one time interval, a body of literature about the female subculture at another point in time, and still a third body of literature at another time dealing with the subculture in juvenile institutions. Research and publications on adult male subcultures preceeded investigations and writings on female mainly to those social scientists researching female institutions and making comparisons by referring to the preexistent and established body of knowledge about male institutions. The observations that we have made thus far in this chapter are gleaned from the two well-known books on female prison subculture: Ward and Kassebaum's *Women's Prison: Sex and Social Structure,* and Giallombardo's *Society of Women: A Study of a Women's Prison.* Both books were researched and written after the appearance of the giants in the male subculture literature: Clemmer's *The Prison Community,* and Sykes'

The Society of Captives. The authors of both female subculture books refer to the established literature about male subcultures in formulating comparisons between the two systems. Some later writers have attempted comparisons by referring to the sources on both male and female subcultures.[7] The overall result is that there is considerable agreement on the reasons for the differences and the conclusions of Ward and Kassebaum and Giallombardo stand largely undisturbed at this point.[8] The essence of their conclusions is that men and women form different social systems in prisons because they were socialized in different ways before they came to prison. The next task is to assess what these differences imply for the nature of sub rosa economic activities in the two systems.

MALE ECONOMIC SYSTEMS:
THE CLIQUE AND ENTREPRENEUR

Sub rosa economic activity in the male prisons centers around either the independent self-producer or the entrepreneurial activities of a clique directed by a leader. Thus one finds the underground business being conducted either by an individual or by a group. Rarely does activity stem from a dyadic form of economic cooperation, even though the free world economy provides many models of such business arrangements in that partnerships are a common form of business organization.

Following the precedents set by the sociologists, preinstitutional experiences may be supposed to supply the models for business arrangements in the prison world. That entrepreneurial activity is organized around the clique rather than the partnership is not odd if one bears in mind the nature of the preinstitution business experience of the clique leader. While there is a tendency for the social typing in the male subculture literature to ascribe separate identities to the right guy leader and the merchant, we have argued throughout this book that the leader is the only inmate powerful enough to be a successful merchant in the system; that, in effect, the emphasis on separating the two roles has caused a degree of confusion.

We do not doubt that the derogatory term merchant is applied to the relatively inept prison character who seems overly mercenary to his associates. However, one must not suppose that the right guy is above operating a prison racket. In fact, his leadership qualities are recognized largely from having wealth and favors to dispense and from providing an avenue of anti-institutional activity as an expression of rebellion. Additionally, the inmate leader has the power and influence to enforce the secrecy necessary for large scale economic activities.

We advance the proposition that the relatively large scale and profit-making economic activity is conducted by cliques under the direction and tutelage of a right guy. Entrepreneurship is merely the organizing of resources for the conduct of economic activity. Unquestionably, it is the influence of the right guy that determines the particular nature of the sub rosa business firm. If the sociologists are correct about the influence of preinstitution life (and we believe that they are correct), then the preinstitution business experience of the right guy social type must be examined to predict the type of business organization that he will conceptualize. In doing so, the research of Clarence Schrag is most helpful: the right guy is the "antisocial inmate" in his terminology. Within the different social types identified by Schrag, he was able to establish definitive patterns of preinstitution experiences associated with each type. His description of the careers of prison right guys (antisocial inmates) is useful for our purposes. Schrag found that the antisocial types were recidivistic from their early youth, advancing from the types of crimes committed by juvenile gangs to the low-skill crimes of burglary, robbery, and assault. These social types *earn a living* by contacts with organized crime. However, Schrag points out that such persons rarely rise to positions of power in their fringe area contacts with organized crime. Once incarcerated, antisocial types continue their life pattern of rebellion against conventional norms.[9]

It is important to note Schrag's emphasis on the inmate rebellion and "opposition to prison authorities," because such anti-institution sentiments are an important motivation in the operation of prison rackets—probably holding equal status with the profit motive. More significantly, the right guy has had the bulk of his business experience with organized crime. While the free world experiences of the right guy do provide his conceptualization of business organization, his preinstitution business experience does not stem from activity in the mainstream economy; rather, it originates in the ghetto dealings of organized crime.

The right-guy-controlled prison clique engaged in prison rackets organizationally resembles the internal structure of the organized crime family. For purposes of comparison, it is useful to consider the internal structure of organized crime groups as reported by the President's Commission on Law Enforcement and Administration of Justice.[10] The Task Force reports the existence of 24 groups, each known as a "family." Each group has from 20 to 700 men in an organization operated with a set of positions designed to maximize profits. Each group has a leader, wielding absolute power, whose function is to maintain order and maximize profits. Each boss has an "underboss" who is, in effect, the vice president. The underboss relays messages to the leader and passes orders down the chain of command; occasionally the underboss will act on behalf of the leader. A *consigliere,* or counselor, is on the same level as the underboss, but he acts in a staff capacity by advising the boss on business matters.

Beneath the underboss is a layer of *caporegimes,* or lieutenants, who, as a form of protection from police intrusions, help the boss to avoid direct contact with the workers. The money, orders, and communications that flow to and fro between the boss and the workers must all come through the lieutenants. Some lieutenants serve as trusted go-betweens while others head operating units. At the lowest level in the structure, one finds the *soldati,* or soldiers, who do the actual work by operating particular illicit enterprises such as loan sharking or gambling operations. Soldiers may work on a commission basis or may own the business and pay a part of the profits to the organization in return for the right to operate.[11]

In considering the operation of the enterprise prison clique, the internal organization is remarkably similar to the organized crime family on the outside. As already mentioned, the right guy clique leader possesses absolute power in respect to the operation of the clique. He receives the profits and arranges for their distribution to clique members after taking his self-appointed share. The right guy has an array of lieutenants who act as buffers between him and the workers and who pass along his orders. These lieutenants appear to serve the same basic purposes as those in the organized crime family: they keep the leader insulated from the prison guards. John C. Watkins, former warden of the Draper Correctional Center in Alabama, has commented on the difficulty of identifying solid convicts (right guys) because they are so proficient in operating in the background and remaining anonymous.[12] In passing, it should be noted that this insulation of the right guy from guards and workers may account for his protection from the derogatory label of "merchant." Like the organized crime boss, the prison clique leader may remain unknown to the soldiers who carry out the orders of the lieutenants. However, the prison community is compact and possesses an efficient grapevine, so it is difficult for the clique leader to remain unknown to the workers in his organization.

In comparing the internal structure of the prison clique with that of the organized crime family, one finds the position of counselor is missing in the prison setting. The absence of that position can be logically accounted for on two bases: first, the prison clique leader's experience with organized crime has been at a rather low level and he, therefore, cannot be expected to know the finer points of upper echelon organization; and second, since the position of counselor is usually occupied by some elderly sage who is semi-retired from crime,[13] he may not be found in the prison setting.

Not only is the internal structure of the prison clique similar to that of organized crime, but the nature of the illicit activities is also notably similar. The Task Force on Organized Crime states that the range of business operations of the organized crime family includes gambling, narcotics, loan sharking, extortion, and alcohol.[14] These "rackets" are the same as the prison rackets noted in earlier chapters. In terms of economic theory, this array of activities is significant. One ordinarily thinks of economic activity originating in response to a demand for certain types of goods and services. In fact, virtually all the sociologists' references to the illicit economic system stress the paucity of goods and prison deprivation as the sole explanation for the demand for illicit goods and services.

While there is substantial truth in the proposition that prison rackets arise in response to demand, that proposition is not a wholly adequate explanation. Economists know that demand can be "created" and, in fact, often is in our society. Consumers are frequently bombarded with advertising when a company begins to market a new product. The company has manufactured a product for which no identifiable demand exists at the time of its production. The demand for the new product is truly created by advertising, which makes the consumer develop or feel a present need of the product or service.

The implication for prison rackets is evident: the enterprising right guy may originate a particular racket simply because he believes that he knows how to operate that racket. Once the racket is created, its end products exist in an economy of scarcity as a supply and can be marketed via subtle bits and pieces of information and advertising. Supply, then, plays a role in prison rackets that is at least as crucial as the role played by demand. Perhaps this procedure is actually a more logical assessment of the nature of prison rackets simply because the assessment of the demand for a product is a complicated process and one could safely assume that the right guy has had no, or scant, previous experience in forecasting demand. Conversely, he has had some, albeit small, experience in operating a racket (creating supply).

In comparing the prison clique with the organized crime family, one final set of functions should be mentioned. The Task Force on Organized Crime notes that organized crime is a unique form of criminal activity because it utilizes the positions of enforcers and corrupters. The position of enforcer entails maintaining organizational integrity by the killing and maiming of reluctant members. The job description of the position of corrupter includes establishing acceptable relations with public officials and other influential persons.[15]

The prison clique is known to use both positions. A prison has an abundance of "outlaws", "dingbats" (asocial inmates) who can be hired as enforcers at relatively reasonable rates. The rat, or informer, is a threat to illicit activities either inside the prison or outside and is frequently the victim of the enforcer. The corrupter role is often vital to the prison clique, since some types of illicit goods such as hard drugs can only be obtained by bribing an official and some types of services such as a change of living quarters can only be provided by corrupting an influential person, perhaps a trusted "square john" type of inmate who controls records. Whereas the right guy almost never does the enforcement work himself, he may undertake the more delicate job of corrupter.

Thus the preinstitution experiences of the inmate determine his choice of business organization and operation just as they determine his choice of social roles to act out in the prison. However, the business experience of the right guy before entering the prison has not been of a garden variety; it is ghetto hustling that forms the basis of his business concepts, rather than mainstream economic activity. Joe Grant, number 1076, was not Pleasant Valley's trusted certified public accountant. The similarity of the business operations of the prison clique and the organized crime family is striking in terms of methods, nature of products and services provided and internal structure. This observation, while not previously noted in the correctional literature, is supported by the general trend of sociological thought, which stresses preinstitution experience as the dominant factor in modes of prison adaptation.

The other type of economic activity in the male prison, the self producer/reciprocal trade variety, is carried on by several of the social types other than the right guy leader. Such small scale economic activity is not entrepreneurially oriented; rather, it is a straightforward attempt to raise living standards above the subsistence level. The bulk of the prisoners have working class backgrounds and have learned handicraft skills that are useful in the building of electric heaters for coffee, homemade hot plates, and weapons. Activities like these, although defined as illicit in the prison setting, are not unlike the activities of a poor man in the free world who makes some efforts to grow or manufacture a few items that his family uses and who undertakes the performance of some services for himself, for example, the repair of his own automobile. In addition, the self-producer, should he have an oversupply, will peddle the extras for a price. The activities of these self-producer type of inmates are also related to their preinstitutional experiences. However, they do not possess the leadership ability to become clique leaders. Lacking the skill, enforcement, and insulation of the clique leaders, some self-producers will make pests of themselves if they are aggressive in trying to market their wares, thus receiving the derogatory title "merchant."

FEMALE ECONOMIC SYSTEM:
FAMILY AND BUTCH/FEMME RELATIONSHIPS

The illicit economic activity in women's prisons occurs mainly within the context of imaginary kinship relationships and the butch/femme liason. Within these structures, production, exchange, and consumption basically take place. Here you also see remnants of entreprenuerial activity. The social structure and activities of female institutions have an obvious impact upon the organization of illicit economic activity.

Looking first at the basic relationship, the "family" composition calls for the casting of some members in breadwinner roles and other members in nonbreadwinner roles and for sharing. One immediately apparent implication is that the creation of nonbreadwinner roles reduces the overall productivity of the female prison population when compared to the male economic structure. Incarcerated females assigned nonbreadwinner roles are "productive" in the sense that they work for the family by providing the housekeeping services, but such provision of services has little significance for the prison staff who are more concerned with illicit economic activity, which presents a real or fancied danger to the security of the institution.

In the male system, the individual is expected to perform his role in the sub rosa economic system *and* attend to his own housekeeping chores by performing them himself or by using the wages from his illicit activities to hire another inmate to perform the chores. Thus the productivity in the male prison is relatively high in that each individual takes care of his own housekeeping and performs additional economic activity in the context of the entrepreneur-directed prison clique or the self producer/reciprocal barter mode of activity. Outside the walls, output per capita of a family would tend to be lower than output per captia of a group of unrelated adult individuals.

The lower productivity of female prisoners due to the division of roles does not necessarily mean that there is a greater paucity of goods in the female institution, because the general trend in American penology has been to provide more of the amenities of life to female than male prisoners through the formal prison economic system. The extra productivity of the male inmates may merely serve to put the availability of goods and services on a par with female prisons. However, it does lead to the projection that the male prison will have a greater intensity of illicit economic activity, due to the need for almost every individual to perform a breadwinning role in the male culture.

The social arrangements in the female prison have an obvious impact on the *organization* of illicit economic activity. In turn, we have seen that the social arrangement culminating in the family structure has its cultural origins in the preinstitution experiences of the inmates. The preinstitution activities of female offenders also have an impact on the *type* of economic activity undertaken. Women who participate in the work force usually are in service oriented occupations where their tasks are an extension of their jobs in the home. While male institutions have a significant amount of value creation in that the inmates manufacture various types of products: appliances, weapons, alcohol, and so on. Manufacturing products from raw materials or waste products creates "value" because the intermediate goods are converted to a desired commodity which did not exist before. The value created can be divided up among the group members according to some distribution scheme which the group agrees upon.

Of course, if the raw materials used in maufacturing must be stolen, the men are not completely self-sufficient and independent. Value creation gives a collection of people more autonomy in that they become less dependent upon other groups for their needs. For example, the collection of people who initially settled the American colonies were extremely dependent upon Britain because little manufacturing was done. Later, when the American colonists began to manufacture vital products, the colonists were able to break away from the mother country and become independent.

The illicit activities of the female prison are oriented more toward the transfer of the ownership of goods. Because of their preinstitutional roles, the female prisoners rely upon shoplifting (boosting) types of activities to obtain extra goods. Shoplifting, or theft, simply transfers ownership of the products and creates time and place utility. The manufacturing that does occur involves skills learned in the home—for example, the making of alcoholic beverages (cooking) and sewing. The implication is that female prisoners are not independent in the economic realm and must depend upon another group—the staff—for the stocking of goods, which can be stolen.

Despite the relatively smaller amount of value creation in the female prison, the inmates would appear to be just as proficient as the males in satisfying their economic needs. Although less skillful in manufacturing than males, the females compensate by becoming more adept than males in the arts of thievery. Here, the implications for rehabilitation are clear. The skill used by the male in conducting illicit economic activity in the prison can be transferred to legitimate manufacturing if his values can be redirected. Conversely, the boosting skills of the female prisoner are obviously less likely to be transferred to legitimate economic roles in the free world. Industry has limited openings for a skilled shoplifter. The female who engages in boosting in prison is simply sharpening criminal talents which have no accepted function in the mainstream of economic life. It appears that female prisons may truly be "schools of crime."

In short, incarcerated females who are assigned "male" bread-winner roles in families react to the role expectations as "females". In other words, preinstitution training in the case of female prisoners leads them to provide some services such as cooking and sewing, but generally to use nonvalue-creating transfer techniques to provide for their families. "Boosting" is a criminal career that does not have entry barriers for women and, consequently, they have gained experience in that mode of obtaining commodities. In prison, such experience is utilized when a woman is called upon to be a provider.

With butch/femme relationships where there are decidedly male and female roles, one finds the booster who is dubbed a "commissary hustler." Again the preinstitutional social and economic experience of inmates is vividly depicted. The commissary hustler has an organization comprised of inmates playing femme roles who pay her tribute and curry her affection with gifts and supplies from the legal and illegal prison economy. Outside, the comparable business is the pander and prostitute organization. Prostitutes pay the pander (pimp) a commission for the various services he performs. It is an odd turn of events that women, when playing the role of men, should assume the economic organization and behavior of a pimp who, besides taking a high commission on all their jobs, alternately shows affection for them, protects them, and beats them up. The pander is not beloved by his employees. It is even more strange that the femmes will let a butch hustle them. Perhaps femmes will accept a butch who is a commissary hustler for the same reasons prostitutes will work for pimps on the outside.

COMPARISON OF SUB ROSA ECONOMIC ACTIVITY

Male prisoners are more prone to manufacturing goods than are female prisoners, who tend to engage in nonbarter transfer of wealth—that is to say, to steal. The male system would seem to have more potential for economic autonomy, but the females compensate for their lack of handicraft-manufacturing experience by refining the thievery skills already possessed. Both systems, on the balance, serve the economic needs of the inmates in question.

To the extent that illicit economic activity serves the psychological need of expressing anti-institutional sentiments, as opposed to the physiological needs of the body, the female system may be superior. Reliance upon theft as the primary mode of obtaining commodities is symbolically more damaging to the prison staff and the society they represent than is the self-reliance demonstrated by using illicit manufacturing as the primary means of obtaining goods. Male inmates express their contempt for the system by "getting away with" forbidden activities. Females express their contempt by directly "taking from" the system. Even so, the difference in techniques is not deliberate, but rather the extension of know-how gained prior to entering the prison.

One clear implication from the differences of the two sub rosa systems is in the nature of staff-directed activities in the prison setting. The skills of the female prisoners often are criminalistic due partly to the occupation entry barriers imposed against women in general. Vocational training is needed and is conducted in both male and female institutions. However, it would appear that female offenders have a greater need for the learning of marketable, legitimate skills, and that relatively more emphasis should be placed on vocational training in female prisons. Conversely, males have a wider array of skills gained from their preinstitution experiences and greater opportunities for entry into training programs or apprenticeship roles once they leave the prison. It may well be that male prisons should emphasize academic training more than vocational training. The reduction of illiteracy in the case of male prisoners would result in more successful job applications which, in turn, would allow the men an opportunity to utilize manual skills already developed.

In this chapter we have discussed some of the basic differences in the social and economic organization of male and female prisons. This concludes the presentation of descriptive material. While this chapter and previous chapters include some analytical material, the primary goal has been to present the raw material. The final chapter is an attempt to put all the information into a conceptual framework, and to draw inferences for correctional practitioners, economists, and other social scientists with an interest in corrections.

Notes to Chapter 5

1. Sykes's summarized list of deprivations is as follows: (1) deprivation of liberty, (2) deprivation of goods and services, (3) deprivation of heterosexual relationships, (4) deprivation of autonomy, and (5) deprivation of security. See: Gresham M. Sykes, *The Society of Captives* (Princeton, N.J: Princeton University Press, 1971), pp. 63-83.

2. David A. Ward and Gene G. Kassebaum, *Women's Prison: Sex and Social Structure* (Chicago: Aldine, 1965), pp. 14-15. Also see: "Lesbian Liasons," *Transaction* 1 (January 1964); 28-32; and "Homosexuality: A Mode of Adaptation in a Prison for Women," *Social Problems* 12 (Fall 1964): 159-177 by the same authors.

3. Ward and Kassebaum, *Women's Prisons,* p. 15.

4. *Ibid.*

5. Rose Giallombardo, *Society of Women: A Study of a Women's Prison* (New york: John Wiley, 1966), pp. 14-17.

6. *Ibid.,* pp. 184-188.

7. *Ibid.,* p. 186. Also see: Rose Giallombardo "Social Roles in a Prison for Women," *Social Problems* 13 (Winter 1966): 268-288.

8. Sheldon Messinger, "Review of *Society of Women: A Study of a Women's Prison* and *Women's Prison: Sex and Social Structure,*" *The American Sociological Review* 32 (February 1967): 143-146.

9. Clarence Schrag, "Some Foundations for a Theory of Correction," in *The Prison: Studies in Institutional Organization and Change,* ed. Donald R. Cressey (New York: Holt, Rinehart and Winston, 1961), pp. 348-349.

10. The President's Commission on Law Enforcement and Administration of Justice, Task Force on Organized Crime, *Task Force Report: Organized Crime* (Washington, D.C: U.S. Government Printing Office, 1967).

11. *Ibid.,* pp. 7-8.

12. John C. Watkins, "The Modification of the Subculture in a Correctional Institution," presented at the 94th Congress of Correction, Kansas City, Missouri, September 1, 1964. (Mimeographed.)

13. Task Force on Organized Crime, p. 8.

14. *Ibid.*

15. *Ibid.*

Chapter Six

Conceptualizing the Illicit Economic System and its Implications

This final chapter consists of three separate, but related, parts. First is some material for the noneconomist that will help him to conceptualize the economic activity discussed as a part of a social system—including some arguments as to the need to be able to do so. The second section is directed toward economists, but is primarily composed of policy decisions as opposed to nuances of theory and should be of interest to correctional practitioners and academicians. The purpose of this section is to draw attention to national economic policy, which should assist in the prevention of crime and reintegration of the convicted into the mainstream of society. The final pages include an assessment of applicable correctional policies.

INTERRELATEDNESS OF SUB ROSA TRANSACTIONS

The correctional officer has a particular view of the types of economic transactions which have been depicted throughout the book. To the correctional practitioner, prison rackets appear and disappear somewhat like brush fires; guards will become aware of the regular occurrence of some illicit activity—a daily dice game in an abandoned coal shed, for example—and will break up the activity, punish the participants, and consider the matter ended until another occasion for discovery of forbidden activities. Such discoveries come when staff members are unusually diligent in the performance of their duties, when inmates get careless, or when an informer notifies the authorities. Thus, staff members see manifestations of sub rosa economic activities in much the same way that a ship's captain sees the tip of an iceberg. Like the ship's captain, who knows that the iceberg is probably much larger than the visible portion, the correctional officer is aware that many forbidden economic transactions must occur without his knowledge. Yet, the officer's view of the illicit activities is a fragmented view; he sees only some individual transactions. It is helpful to consider the interrelatedness of the transactions and to be able to conceptualize them as a system.

Probably the easiest way to begin is to start with the individual transaction. Suppose that Convict Helbig has his heart set on obtaining a change in the assignment of his living quarters. Helbig approaches Convict Ingrate, a clerk in the administrative offices, because Helbig has heard that Ingrate can arrange changes in living quarters for a price. Ingrate is amenable to the idea and Helbig pays Ingrate two cartons of cigarettes for the service. This exchange is a simple transaction: Helbig has paid two cartons of cigarettes to Ingrate in exchange for a favor. Suppose temporarily that the prison guards had detected this illicit transaction and had intervened. The tendency of the guards would be to concentrate on the transaction as an isolated incident, to gather the facts for presentation to the disciplinary committee, and, perhaps, to watch Helbig and Ingrate more carefully. If the guards were in a thoughtful mood, they might have momentarily speculated about how Helbig obtained the two cartons of cigarettes and about the possible disposition that Ingrate would make of the smokes. In such speculation the answers would seem to be obvious: Helbig could certainly have legally purchased the cigarettes at a previous visit to the prison commissary. As to the disposition of the cigarettes, obviously Ingrate could intend to smoke the cigarettes. If the transaction is viewed in this casual manner, the observer could not visualize an economic *system* supporting the single event of the transaction.

Suppose now that the transaction in question was not detected and interrupted by the guards. Additional illicit transactions could conceivably occur in the following order. Ingrate accepts the two cartons of cigarettes from Helbig, but has no intention of smoking them. Two days later, Ingrate takes the two original cartons of cigarettes and gives them to Convict Jonesy. Jonesy is a loan shark and Ingrate is applying the cigarettes to the payment of a debt he owes Jonesy. Although the same two cartons of cigarettes are involved, two illicit transactions have now occured. Jonesy, however, does not intend to smoke the cigarettes either. Jonesy has a bad debt outstanding and is concerned lest the deadbeat set a dangerous precedent of not paying promptly. Thus, Jonesy contracts with Convict Killer to rough up the deadbeat in return for two cartons of cigarettes. Some time later, the deadbeat has gotten the message and the original two cartons of cigarettes are passed along from Jonesy to Killer. At this point, three illicit transactions have occurred involving a total payment of six cartons of cigarettes. Even so, the two original cartons are actually only changing hands.

Killer, not having a smoking habit, has no intention of consuming the cigarettes either. Let us suppose that Killer keeps a "boy" as a cellmate. The boy, whose real name is Lloyd, regularly receives "favors" from Killer for the services he performs in the not-so-dead of night. On this occasion, Killer gives the two cartons of cigarettes to Convict Lloyd. Lloyd, who feels that he must look nice for Killer's sake, also has expenses. Lloyd has a contract with one of the laundry workers and regularly pays the worker two cartons of cigarettes per month in return for special laundry services. Thus the original two cartons of cigarettes are turned over to the laundry worker in the fifth illicit transaction of this series. At the completion of the fifth transaction, it is obvious that the series now involves the total payments of ten cartons of cigarettes. Having followed the series of transactions carefully, it is also obvious that only the original two cartons of cigarettes were used to effect the five transactions.

Where does the series stop? The answer is that it does not stop. Thus far, we have traced this imaginary series of transactions in a straight line from Helbig to Ingrate to Jonesy to Killer to Lloyd to the unidentified laundry worker. Let us now imagine a circle instead of a straight line. This can be done by arranging the cast of characters in a circle and by specifying that the unidentified laundry worker is Helbig. By finding that the laundry worker is really Helbig, we can make an excellent guess as to how he received the original two cartons of cigarettes before our imaginary series of trans- actions began: he probably received them in payment for performing special laundry services.

Since we have supposed that the original two cartons of cigarettes have flowed from hand to hand until they have ultimately returned to the first person in the series, it is easy to see that Helbig is now in a position to initiate a second series of illicit transactions. The circular flow of economic activity depicted in the first series of transactions can be theoretically illus- trated by simply tracing the original cigarettes through a second round of transactions with the same cast of characters. For example, Helbig has discovered that his new living arrangements are not as satisfactory as he believed they would be and must pay Ingrate two cartons of cigarettes to change him back to his first cell. Ingrate still owes a debt to Jonesy and is still passing on most of his income to Jonesy, who finds that he must hire Killer again because he has another deadbeat on his hands. Killer, of course, is still periodically giving favors to Lloyd, who, in turn, finds that another month has passed and that it is time to pay his laundry bill to Helbig. After the second series of transactions, we find that a total of ten illicit exchanges have occurred involving a total payment of twenty cartons of cigarettes. At the same time, we find that only two cartons of cigarettes were actually needed to effect all the economic activity stretching over a two-month interval.

This fanciful account of economic transactions is imaginary only because it has been greatly simplified to demonstrate the interrelatedness of economic transactions. Economic activity is often depicted as a circular flow of transaction. What is meant by a "circular flow of economic activity" is that there are two views of any one transaction. If we break into the chain of events being depicted—let us say with Jonesy—we find that Jonesy's view of his payment to Killer is that the two outgoing cartons of cigarettes represent an "expense." However, from Killer's viewpoint, his receipt of the two cartons of cigarettes represents "income." Two facts become apparent: (1) the cigarettes being used as a form of money are of secondary importance in the series of transactions, while the services being provided are of primary importance; and (2) the transactions are indicative of a relatively complex economic system and are not simple barter transactions.

In a simple barter transaction, Helbig might provide Ingrate with two cartons of cigarettes in return for the desired change of scenery. Ingrate, a heavy smoker, simply consumes the two cartons of cigarettes. If such were the case, there would be no "series" of transactions; rather, there would be only the one exchange in which Helbig received full satisfaction in the form of a service and Ingrate received full satisfaction in the form of consumption. In such a simple barter transaction, the cigarettes would be considered as a product (consumer goods) instead of being considered as money. Furthermore, once the cigarettes were consumed, there could be no additional transactions such as those depicted in the series.

The descriptive material in the earlier chapters demonstrates that there are two forms of transactions in the sub rosa economic system of the prison. The simple barter transaction is demonstrated by that which we have called "self-producers and reciprocal trade." The more complex series of transactions is demonstrated by that which we have called "entrepreneurial activity." The significance of the distinction between the two forms of activity will be clarified in the following sections. For now, it is important to be able to visualize the series, or circular flow, of sub rosa activity.

IMPORTANCE OF INTERRELATED TRANSACTIONS

From the viewpoint of correctional practitioners, the importance of understanding the interrelatedness of the economic transactions is related to the custody and the treatment goals of the institution. The importance of such understanding for custody goals is the more obvious and will be discussed first.

Custody involves preventing escapes, keeping contraband out of the prison, and keeping peace among the inmates. A knowledge of the nature of sub rosa economic activity is useful in accomplishing all three of these goals. Successful escape, or a planned escape that the inmate believes will be successful, requires the support of certain economic resources. Cash will be needed, as will civilian clothing. We have used a number of illustrations from Malcolm Braly's novel because his main character, Chilly Willy, provides excellent illustrations of how cash and civilian clothing can be obtained through the application of entrepreneurial ability.

Chilly Willy was "poor" when he entered the prison because he was not allowed to bring any material goods into the prison with him. Even so, the prison officials could not prevent him from bringing in his street skills—entrepreneurial ability, if you will. The meager resources that he could legally acquire from the formal prison economic system would have been perpetually inadequate for obtaining such expensive contraband as cash and civilian clothing. Had he not developed the entrepreneurial skill to "invest" his small capital in illicit economic activity supported by the inmate culture, valuable contraband would have been outside his reach. By gambling shrewdly, Willy gradually accumulated a quantity of cigarettes (representing money in the sub rosa system) with which he was able to buy cash (a commodity in the sub rosa system).

With the accumulation of cash, Willy became a special threat to the goal of custody in a number of ways. With cash, Willy could have obtained civilian clothing by purchasing garments that had been stolen by inmates or by corrupting a low-paid guard. Thus Willy could have had the two essential ingredients for successful escape—money and clothing—through the application of his entrepreneurial skill—although the novelist, Braly, did not provide his character, Willy, with a desire to escape.

The novel does depict other types of threats to the custody goal which were posed by Willy's unexpected and illicit prosperity. Willy's entre-preneurial accumulation of wealth made him powerful within the inmate society. The novel illustrates his use of his wealth in corrupting a guard into bringing *contraband* into the prison in the form of drugs and also depicts his power to add to the insecurity of institution life in that he paid a mentally disturbed inmate to attack another inmate who was hopelessly indebted to Willy. All the destruction and all the potential havoc within Willy's grasp came about because of his accumulation of wealth via illegal means.

Wealth, and the power that follows wealth, can be obtained within the sub rosa economic system of the prison by application of entrepreneurial ability—especially if the prison has a strong anti-institution subculture that operates to hold down the activities of rats. A large amount of illicit entre-preneurial activity requires secrecy, and secrecy can only be obtained to the extent that inmates remain loyal to the convict code. Wealth and power gained by antisocial inmate leaders will pose a significant threat to the custody goal of a prison because they provide the wherewithal to obtain the instruments of escape, the means for bringing contraband into the prison, and the means of creating violence within the prison population.

What the existence of the sub rosa economic system implies for the achievement of the custody goals of a prison is a complicated question. One can take either a narrow and short range approach or one can consider the issue from a broader and long range view. Further on in this chapter we will make some recommendations for a long range solution to the problem created by the illicit economic system. However, let us now deal with the more narrow and short run approach, since hundreds of correctional officers find that they must work in existing prisons with current correctional policies while awaiting substantive implementation of correctional reform.

Training

Taking a short run approach to the problems created by the illicit economic system in prisons, we recommend that correctional officers be given some training that will make them aware of the interrelatedness of illicit economic transactions, for the purpose of better achieving the custody goals of the prison. Their training need not be elaborate or expensive or time consuming. Awareness of the principles delineated in the first part of this chapter would be sufficient knowledge for correctional officers to enable them to detect many more prison rackets. These principles are the concept of a *flow* of economic activity, the conceptualization of economic activity as a *circular* flow, and the two-sided nature of transactions.

These principles are among the very simpliest in economic theory and could be conveyed to a new group of correctional officers within a one-hour training period. And the awareness of a sub rosa economic system would enable the officers to detect its manifestations much more easily. Having studied the illicit system ourselves, we find that we are now able to detect irregularities even on brief tours of prison facilities. For example, one sees most of the inmates going to the dining hall for a meal, but one notices that one inmate finds it unnecessary to eat the main-line food and is, instead, buying his meal at the prison commissary. One wonders how the inmate can afford to pass up free food and "eat out." It may well be that he is extensively involved in a prison racket. This is but one example of how an awareness of the nature of the operation of a sub rosa economy can assist an officer in achieving the custody function of the institution.

Implications for Rehabilitation

Let us turn now to the implications of the sub rosa economic system for the institution goal of rehabilitation. The word "rehabilitation," as it is applied to the inmates of prisons, means simply that the aim of the institution is to release inmates who will not commit other crimes, which will cause them to be sent back to the institution. In general, the recidivism rate is usually estimated to be in the neighborhood of 60 to 70 percent and this rather high failure rate is commonly blamed on prisons.

Prison programs aimed at achieving the goal of rehabilitation involve two broad spectrums of activity: (1) use of therapists, generally trained in psychology, in an attempt to bring about a change in the inmate's attitudes toward society to enable him to function in the free society; and (2) academic and vocational training to raise the skills of the inmate to a level where he can function in the economic system of the free society. In both spectrums of rehabilitation efforts, the existence of the sub rosa economic system is a detriment to the goals sought by the prison. The distinction that we have made between simple barter transactions and entrepreneurial activity is helpful in understanding the rehabilitation implications posed by the operation of the sub rosa economy.

The motivation for simple barter transactions is natural and harmless—not a threat to the rehabilitation goals of the institution. The circumstances of life within the walls impose an artifical scarcity upon the individuals who are incarcerated. Their motivation for the initiation of simple barter transactions is a basic desire to improve their material resources and to make their lives a tiny bit more comfortable. This type of motivation cannot be conceived to be harmful to the rehabilitation goals of the prison and is probably not a threat to the custody goals of the institution. In fact, one would tend to doubt that a person could be rehabilitated if he were so lethargic or so withdrawn that he was not interested in attempting to better his condition.

However, the type of illicit transactions that we have designated as entrepreneurial activity pose a different problem for the goal of rehabilitation. To some extent, the motivation for entrepreneurial activity is the same as the motivation for simple barter transactions: the inmate wants to expand his material resources. But the motivation for entrepreneurial activity is much more complex. As we have pointed out, the business techniques of the prison entrepreneur are geared to his preinstitution experiences—drawing upon the techniques of organized crime rather than the techniques of legitimate business. These counter-culture activities are, in all likelihood, the cause of the inmate's incarceration.

We have demonstrated that the prison entrepreneur is the social type known as a right guy, solid convict, or antisocial inmate. He is not the less prestigious "merchant," as one would expect from reading the existing body of literature on inmate culture. As an inmate leader, the prison entrepreneur has motivations beyond the simple desire to better his material well-being. Sociological research has shown that this antisocial type of inmate has a lifelong pattern of rebellion and antiestablishment activities. His business techniques and motivations are a part of the pattern of rebellion he has brought to the prison with him and that he will take with him when he again returns to the free society. In the free world, he was a small fish in a big pond because he had petty positions with organized crime. In the prison he becomes a big fish in a small pond, because his illicit entrepreneurial skills are outstanding in a world of blunderers and incompetents. Using the illicit business tactics of organized crime, the prison entrepreneur verbally expresses his antisocial feelings with slogans such as "only suckers work," or in the more colorful language of Braly's prison entrepreneur: "Think of all them fools out there bustin' their asses so them bitches can sit under those hair dryers, . . . "[1]

Prison entrepreneurial activity, we maintain, is a threat to the rehabilitation goals of the prison because it has as its primary motivation the continuation and expansion of rebellion against society. The techniques are illegitimate, but workable, and each success reinforces the antiestablishment determination of the prison entrepreneurs; each success further convinces them that it is foolish and futile to even attempt to change their way of life. This reinforcement of antiestablishment views is powerful enough to counteract any and all efforts by therapists to change the attitudes of such inmates. Furthermore, the reinforcement is a threat to rehabilitation efforts built around academic and vocational training. Such training can only hope to give the inmate a choice of occupations when he leaves the prison: that is, it hopes to enable him to make more money working as a barber or automobile mechanic than he can by burglarizing homes or robbing service stations. The average burglar or armed robber does not find his crimes to be very lucrative.

Obviously, the successes of the prison entrepreneur who is becoming relatively wealthy via illegitimate means will reaffirm his conviction that legitimate means are for "suckers." Female prisoners, who were being taught to do industrial sewing, have been known to say that they had no intention of slaving for a week to earn the wages of a seamstress when they could make a similar amount on Saturday night by engaging in prostitution. This statement illustrates the futility of supplying academic and vocational training to persons who hold firmly to a belief in the efficacy of illegitimate norms. Understanding the antiestablishment bias that is continually reinforced by successful prison entrepreneurship is vital to the development of strategies for rehabilitation. We will return to this topic later in this chapter when discussing implications for correctional policy.

IMPLICATIONS FOR ECONOMIC POLICY

Economic theory can be used to formulate economic policy for dealing with social problems when a socially controllable variable can be located. In other words, in assessing economic relationships, economists sometimes locate a point in these relationships where one can break into the process and change the structural relationships, with the result that the system in question operates a little more the way society wants it to work. This study is probably too narrow in scope for us to try to draw inferences for broad national economic policy to deal with the criminal justice system. However, the study does suggest certain types of policy recommendations, some of which have received support from other quarters and some of which are our own variations of recommendations that have been proposed for broader based social problems.

One particular problem has caught our attention more than others while we engaged in the research for this book. Prison entrepreneurs have the power to disrupt the operation of the prison because of their leadership talent, their ability to muster wealth and the power that follows it, and their firm allegiance to antisocial values. Their entrepreneurial skills, as demonstrated by sociological research, were used for illegitimate means during their criminal career *before* they entered prison. They have a well defined pattern of progressing from truancy, to expressive theft in boy-gangs, to instrumental theft involving fences for stolen merchandise, and of finally extending their career's in the unsophisticated street crimes such as burglary. The types of crimes that they commit are among those tabulated in the FBI Index of Crimes—those that are annually presented to Americans as evidence of the rising crime rate.

Furthermore, the same sociological research shows that these offenders are highly recidivistic, which means that they continue the same pattern of criminal career *after* leaving the prison until they are eventually caught, convicted, and sentenced to prison for a second time and, ultimately, for a third, fourth, or fifth time. Although their number is small in relation to the total population of the United States, they account for a disproportionate share of street crimes committed and for a disproportionate share of the vast amount of economic resources expended on the operation of the criminal justice system.

There is some evidence that such offenders can be converted to prosocial types—which, in effect, is rehabilitation of the offender. However, by the time the offender reaches an institution where he can be subjected to treatment, he has already done considerable damage to society. Even then, there is certainly no assurance that he can be changed at the institutionalized stage in his career. We will draw some inferences concerning treatment strategies in the next section of this chapter; however, we wish to concentrate now on economic policy, which has the potential for intervention into the antisocial type's career long before he reaches prison.

Most people will agree that devoting resources to the prevention of crime is a more efficient use of our resources than the expensive efforts to deter crime, apprehend criminals, and prosecute and incarcerate persons for long periods of time. The problem is that little is known about how to prevent crime. It seems unlikely that any measure will serve to prevent all types of crimes—that a number of yet-to-be-discovered preventive measures will be required to deal with the broad spectrum of activities defined as criminal in our society. Yet, our society must start somewhere if it is to ever make progress toward meaningful crime prevention; and the life pattern of the antisocial offender suggests a viable area where economic policy can make a contribution in this respect.

A portion of the body of theories on criminology (the causes of crime) suggests that crime is environmentally determined; it is a by-product of urban slums and poverty conditions with the attending breakup of the traditional family structure. This view, although not verified to any great extent in the correctional literature, appears to be rather widely accepted in that popular magazines and representatives of the news media help to promote the idea. Economists involved in policy making are among those who have accepted this view of the environmental determination of criminal activity, so that economic policies aimed at eliminating poverty and ghettoes are seen to have the reduction of crime as one major outcome.

We basically concur with the idea that crime can be reduced by elimination of poverty and ghettoes. However, we would qualify our agreement by noting that the crime reduction impact of the elimination of poverty and ghettoes would be limited to a portion of some categories of crimes. The crime reduction would occur primarily in the unsophisticated street crimes committed by the antisocial types. But to say that crime can be prevented by elimination of poverty and ghettoes is to invite inaction on the part of policy makers in the field of corrections, who have no control over economic policies that reduce poverty.

Economists cannot agree on the best means of eliminating poverty and, even if they could agree, their recommendations must be implemented by politicians, who may not find it expedient to do so (the poor are not politically powerful). Thus we are convinced that the general proposition of reducing crime by eliminating poverty, while commendable, is too general to be useful at this point and may even invite inaction in the criminal justice field if the correctional policy makers become convinced that they must wait until the poverty problem is solved before it will be possible to solve the crime problem. What is needed, we believe, is a modest start, which is more narrowly conceived than an overall poverty reduction effort. The advantages of a more narrow approach are that it can be implemented immediately without devoting overwhelming amounts of resources to the effort, and the payoff will be both quick and substantial.

Our proposed solution is to eliminate employment entry barriers for ghetto residents. Our study convinces us, and other studies corroborate this view,[2] that ghetto hustling (the type of activity that later becomes prison entrepreneurship) is a way of adjustment to life in the ghetto where the residents are shut off and denied meaningful access to the mainstream economy. In fact, the New York State Special Commission on Attica noted that some prisoners perceived that prison life was really an extension of life in the ghetto—that they must continue to use their hustling skills inside the prison for their personal survival just as they had used them in their preinstitution experiences.[3]

Prison life is structured to deny the inmates access to legitimate economic means for satisfying their physiological and psychological wants; but, more significantly, the American economic system in general is also so structured. These antisocial types are familiar to economists as the hard core unemployed, but they are the more successful members of the hard core unemployed who have had the personal initiative to employ their entrepreneurial skills in illegitimate means in order to adjust to a life where they either must suffer the deprivations and stigma of poverty or else become criminals.

If our recommendation for reducing crime by reducing entry barriers to employment is of any value, it must follow that gainful employment does reduce ghetto hustling activities. There is some important evidence that employment does reduce hustling—documentation that is emerging from studies of the job training efforts of the 1960s. At the time of this writing, government manpower training programs, as they developed within the framework of the War on Poverty, are being declared a failure by the Nixon Administration and it appears that these programs will be phased out. The basic problem with the government directed manpower training programs, it seems, is that the programs provided training but no jobs.

In a more optimistic vein, some of the job training efforts of the late 1960s did produce some encouraging results. These were the programs of the National Association of Businessmen (NAB) wherein participating businesses undertook to recruit, train and employ persons considered to be unemployable. Government participated by providing a subsidy that compensated the businesses for the extra expense of training persons who had poor educational and employment backgrounds. The subsidies also served to compensate businesses for the low initial productivity of workers employed through the program.

Of the studies emerging from the NAB effort, at least one deals directly with the basic issue that we are presently concerned with—whether employment reduces hustling activity. The research that addresses the question is Harold Padfield and Roy Williams's *Stay Where You Are: A Study of Unemployables in Industry*. This book is a case study of the NAB project conducted in a San Diego aircraft plant. Their goal in conducting the case study was to produce a sociological and anthropological assessment of the effects of job creation. Chapter Five of the book is devoted to a consideration of "Crime As Revolution."[4] The chapter deals with ghetto hustling as a means of adjusting to life in a substratum where the members are shut out from effective participation in the mainstream economy. They explicitly raised the question of the impact of job creation on the reduction of hustling.

Their findings are encouraging, since they do show that the unemployables in the program gradually tended to give up their hustling activities as they became entrenched in the mainstream economic action of the plant. It must be noted that the Padfield and Williams's research was a case study and hence involves a very small number of workers. The sample size is small, but the inferences to be drawn from it support the a priori position found in both the body of economic literature and correctional literature—that the removal of entry barriers to employment reduces the environmental stresses on the individual that sometimes result in criminogenic actions.

Recommendation

In terms of economic policy directed at crime prevention, we recommend that the NAB program be resurrected and expanded as a deliberate and long range measure for the reduction of ghetto hustling. The original NAB program was a unique product of the times. It arose in a wartime economy wherein the labor supply was short and businessmen were eager to get extra workers even if they had to make unusual efforts to recruit them. Government, too, was eager to expand the labor force to reduce inflationary pressure caused by bottlenecks in the labor supply. Under these favorable conditions the NAB program was conceived and born. As might have been predicted, the NAB program died quietly with the onslaught of the recession in 1970 when business firms began laying off workers and government became less pessimistic about the inflation problem.

In order to have, an impact on crime, the resurrected NAB program must not be allowed to fluctuate with the business cycle; rather, society must be committed to continuing it in prosperity or recession by providing government subsidies to retain unemployables recruited in prosperity if necessary and to continue the recruiting and training of unemployables when business is slack as well as during prosperity. This would, of course, result in higher government expenditures when the economy was slack. Thus the measure could be conceived of as a fiscal policy measure designed to add stimulation to a sluggish economic system. It could, if structured carefully, become one of the automatic stabilizers in our economic system. The continuing recruitment and training of unemployables would, in addition to reducing certain types of crime, have the economic benefit of increasing productivity and breaking down structural unemployment. With increased productivity of workers and elimination of specific bottlenecks in the labor force, a possible spinoff benefit will be relief of some inflationary pressure as the number employed increases.

The policy that, we are proposing is tantamount to making the government the employer of last resort, but only indirectly, since the government would be subsidizing private enterprise for employing workers rather than employing them itself. If we adopted the national policy of making the federal government the employer of last resort by direct employment of workers who could not otherwise find a job, we would be committing ourselves to providing government work for persons throughout their lifetime—a policy that would be a potentially heavy burden to the taxpayers. Conversely, subsidizing the recruitment and training of unemployables in private industry is not a lifelong commitment to provide work. The short-lived NAB program of the late 1960s taught us that although it is difficult to recruit and train unemployables, those who are retained by the participating companies quickly become productive and valuable employees of the firms.

One would project that the expense of recruitment and special training of unemployables would ultimately be greatly reduced since their numbers are relatively small in relation to the size of our total labor force. The expense incurred in retaining such employees during a recession—assuming that government subsidy would be necessary to induce companies to retain them—would be considerable. However, a sluggish economy, given our commitment to maintaining high levels of employment as expressed in the Employment Act of 1946, calls for the federal government to engage in deficit spending in time of recession to stimulate the economy. Deficit spending, under conditions of excessive unemployment, is a proper fiscal policy measure to alleviate the downturn in economic activity. From the point of view of the taxpayer, deficit spending has the advantage of being financed by means other than increases in the rates of taxation.

There are those, economists who oppose any proposal that extends government action into new arenas of endeavor. The basis of their objection is that any extension of government power is more or less a decrease in individual freedom and that it hampers the operation of the free enterprise system. Not belonging to that school of thought, it has always been difficult for us to grasp the logic of their eighteenth century liberalism. However, we are aware of their philosophical position sufficiently to anticipate that such objections to our proposal will be raised. In answer to these anticipated questions, we propose that crime and poverty—not government intervention in the economy—are the social factors that limit freedom. For those in poverty, their alternatives are so hemmed in and limited by their environment that "freedom" is nothing more than a vague and meaningless abstraction. For those above the poverty line, crime creates fear and insecurity that can be regarded as a limit to individual freedom. In short, extension of government intervention into the economy, we feel, is a limitation on individual freedom that exists only on a highly abstract and philosophical plane, if at all. Such abstract discussions of limits to freedom have a place in advanced university seminars, but they have little meaning on the streets where poverty and crime are taking their daily toll. Even if one maintains that our proposed additional commitment for government intervention represents a form of encroachment on individuality, we would suggest that the alternative, tolerating unemployment and crime, represents a greater encroachment.

In conceiving of our recommendation to resurrect the NAB program as a method of preventing crime and *as a measure of fiscal policy,* there arises one major problem. The skills of government and corporate economists are such that determining the proper level of government subsidy to the firm for recruiting, training, and compensation for reduced initial productivity would be relatively simple. More difficult would be the task of deciding the appropriate sums to pay companies, given that an economic recession was under way and the subsidy was designed to motivate companies to retain workers who would otherwise be laid off with a business slowdown. Certainly, some former unemployables would have become productive and valuable employees by the beginning of the recession, but companies would likely be prone to extort subsidies from the government by threatening to lay off the workers. The outcome, one supposes, would be an overpayment to business firms under conditions of recession.

However, viewed as expansionary fiscal policy, an overpayment might well be desirable under these conditions. Previously, expansionary fiscal policy measures have been indirect, in that the federal government has either injected money into the economy in order to induce the business sector to expand (hire more workers) or employ additional workers on public projects. A subsidy designed to prevent the layoff of workers seems to be a more direct approach to the problem—an approach that will produce faster results. Layoffs aggravate a worsening economic outlook because those workers laid off have drastically curtailed incomes, and necessarily lessen their spending—which results in a decrease in aggregate demand, inventory buildup at retail outlets, cutbacks in orders to factories, and, consequently, more layoffs of workers as factory orders decline. A more effective means of employing expansionary fiscal policy should be to avoid layoffs in the first instance, because, hopefully, the downturn would be halted before it became so severe that massive doses of deficit spending on the part of government were required to reverse the process.

In short, we believe that a resurrected and expanded NAB program, receiving a long term commitment and adequate support, would reduce certain types of crimes and would also reduce the social ills associated with poverty for at least a few of those thousands of Americans who suffer the consequences of poverty without turning to crime. Furthermore, it would develop a hitherto untried fiscal policy tool that has the potential of becoming one of our more effective automatic stabilizers.

IMPLICATIONS FOR CORRECTIONAL POLICY

Prison entrepreneurship is expensive for prisons to deal with because a substantial amount of manpower must be devoted to achieving the custody goals of preventing escapes, keeping peace among the inmates, and keeping down contraband. Prison entrepreneurship or hustling is a detriment to achieving all these facets of the custody function, as has been pointed out. We have recommended as a short run solution that correctional officers be given a modicum of training, which will provide knowledge of the nature of the sub rosa economic system and better equip the officers for control of the illicit activities. A long range solution requires policy changes that will alter the system.

To visualize the key variables that can be controlled to reduce prison hustling, it is useful to break down its causation into two separate fractions. One element in the motivation of prison entrepreneurs is a simple and straightforward inducement understood by everyone: the drive to overcome the paucity of one's environment; or, in even simpler terms, the desire to improve one's living standard. On a policy level, the type of attack that can be launched on that problem is not mysterious. Inmates expect to work while they are incarcerated, and do work in the prison industries. However, their poverty is not alleviated by their productive efforts because they are paid nominal sums such as twenty or thirty cents per hour. Throughout our correctional history, prison labor has been restricted by laws written partially by businessmen who fear that prisons will use cheap labor to build and market products, thus engaging in "unfair" competition. Organized labor has demanded "protective" laws that prohibit the paying of market wages to inmates on the basis that they would be taking jobs from "honest" men who "deserve" them.

The correctional literature has various proposals for paying inmate labor the full value of their productive efforts—along with some compelling reasons for doing so. One argument advanced is that inmates paid the full value for their effort could reduce welfare costs by continuing to support their families during incarceration, while at the same time retaining the self-respect and sense of family responsibility that results from being the family breadwinner. These pleas and arguments have largely been ignored, but they continue. We note that the National Council on Crime and Delinquency is preparing a policy statement at the time of this writing. The new NCCD policy statement will recommend that "Inmates who are regularly employed at productive work in federal, state, or local institutions should receive compensation for their labor at a rate no less than the minimum wage standard operative in their state."[5]

The NCCD policy position appears to be a compromise that is politically expedient. Due to the organized labor and business opposition, it seems unlikely that our prison administrators will be able to adopt a policy of paying inmates the full value of their labor. The NCCD proposal is somewhat more modest and may have a reasonable chance of being adopted in the near future. We would lend our support to the NCCD position on the theory that half a loaf is better than none. While the minimum wage is a modest sum, it is still a princely price when compared to the ususal amount paid to inmates. It is, we believe, a sufficient sum to enable the inmate to satisfy pressing needs by legitimate means rather than being forced to turn to illegitimate means.

Some inmates, of low mentality and low productivity, are not going to be worth the minimum wage. However, other inmates are capable and productive workers—worth more than the minimum wage. Overall, the incompetents and the competents might well balance out so that the inmate labor force as a whole would be receiving about what its labor is worth. Such an equalization of pay represents a theme found in socialism, but socialism is hardly a concern in the closed authoritarian society of a prison.

A wage that provides the inmate with the legitimate means for purchasing such simple necessities as toilet articles would reduce hustling to the extent that it is based on the desire to raise oneself slightly above the level of abject poverty. We have noted that the cause of prison hustling can be broken down into two separate parts; the first, a simple desire to raise one's living standard, can be dealt with by adopting the NCCD policy or a similar measure that will allow inmates to earn enough money to attend to their most pressing needs and to perceive that work can be rewarding. The second cause of hustling is more complex because it involves psychic as well as biological needs.

We have indicated that prison entrepreneurship is motivated more by the desire to express anti-institutional sentiments than it is by simple need of goods and services. The complexities of human motivation are not new to economists, for they have studied the behavior of successful businessmen and have found that increased income and wealth were only a part of their drive for success. It is not surprising that prison entrepreneurs likewise have complex economic motivation that extends beyond the desire to add to their wealth. Nor are the psychological facets of their motivation mysterious when viewed within the total context of the inmate culture.

An economic system is not an entity unto itself. It is always a necessary and supporting part of a society. It is a means to an end rather than an end in itself. In the inmate culture of the prison, the sub rosa economic system represents, in a sense, a look at the social arrangements that involve activity having economic implications. The activities having economic implications are a part of the total range of social activities directed toward achieving the implicit or explicit goals of that particular society.

As a viable part of the inmate culture, the sub rosa economic system of the prison assists in achieving the overall goals of the inmate informal organization by providing the necessary resources and the most visible and tangible evidences of the culture. From the viewpoint of the inmates who support a strong inmate culture, the tangible results of the illicit economic system may be the most valued feature of the sub rosa arrangements. Given the tenets of the inmate culture, most investigators are convinced that it exists as an expression of counter-establishment activity, that it can only serve the purpose of uniting the inmates in their struggle to reject their rejectors and to achieve a degree of autonomy and self-respect systematically denied to them by the organizational structure of a prison, which focuses most of its effort on custody.

In terms of correctional policy that will reduce the entrepreneurial hustling—the serious prison rackets—it would seem that the measures that would weaken the inmate culture as an effective vehicle of counter culture activity would also virtually eliminate the prison entrepreneurial activity. The question is, then, what does weaken the inmate culture? We have discussed one approach to weakening the inmate culture at the end of Chapter 2 when we demonstrated how one correctional practitioner has been able to use a blend of psychological techniques and sociological theory to deliberately manage the inmate culture. Warden John C. Watkins has shown us that it can be accomplished, but that it takes great personal skill and dedication to do so. Lacking a warden with such a high level of ability and determination, one might ask what other alternative methods are available to deal with the negative aspects of the inmate social system?

The correctional literature does contain clues that indicate a policy direction that would weaken the inmate culture without the necessity of depending entirely upon one key man such as Warden Watkins. Bernard B. Berk, in a study of three different prisons, concluded that the basic condition generating oppositional informal organizations is an excessive focus on the custody function of the prison, with a corresponding neglect of the treatment function.[6] This study included one prison that was oriented toward treatment, one that was primarily a custody prison, and one that fell somewhere in between the two extremes. In the treatment institution, Berk found that inmate leadership in their informal social system was more centralized than in the others. In the custody institution, and in general, inmates expressed negative attitudes toward the staff and the goals of the institution.[7] Conversely, the inmates in the treatment oriented institution had more positive attitudes toward the goals of the institution, and the informal inmate leadership was more diffused.[8]

In terms of the problem at hand—the reduction of prison entrepreneurial activity—Berk's conclusions would seem to point the way toward policy shifts that would alleviate the problem. In custody grading of prisons, the maximum security institution is presumed to be properly suited for an emphasis on custody as opposed to treatment. In the process of central classification (deciding in what type of prison a newly convicted inmate should be confined), the long term prisoner is believed to be a high escape risk and is sent to the maximum security prison. It does not logically follow that the maximum security prison should serve merely as a warehouse for the inmates considered to be nonrehabilitable, but, in practice, the function of the maximum security institution is often almost solely a holding place.

Berk's research would seem to indicate that a policy of giving maximum security prisons a more treatment oriented atmosphere—to the extent that a treatment mileau is possible given the architecture of such places—would weaken the inmate culture, and, we would maintain, eliminate much of the prison entrepreneurial activity.

To some extent, correctional practice is moving in the direction that we are recommending. For example, the new federal maximum security prison at Marion, Illinois, is visualized as a "therapeutic community" and does apparently have more of a treatment orientation than Alcatraz, the prison it replaced. The Federal Bureau of Prisons is taking its customary leadership role in giving high-risk offenders a place in a treatment oriented institution. In addition to the treatment mileau at the new Marion Penitentiary, the federal system has the new John F. Kennedy Youth Center at Morgantown, West Virginia. The treatment program at the Center is both innovative and extensive.[9] These institutions are considered to be models for future institutional corrections programs even though the correctional literature is promoting a new stance which would rely more on community-based treatment programs and less on institutions. Nonetheless, most people concerned with corrections believe that some prisons will be necessary in the foreseeable future—that some part of the offender population will, of necessity, have to be incarcerated. To the extent that society does continue to use institutional correctional programs, the people in the field will continue to be concerned with reform of the system and the development of new techniques that will foster the basic expressed commitment to the therapeutic philosophy.

Final Recommendation

As a final recommendation, we urge that correctional personnel develop programs and techniques carrying a greater reliance upon policy as opposed to casework. We have no desire to denigrate the valuable contributions of persons who skillfully employ the casework technique—focusing upon the individual or the small group. For some highly proficient caseworkers, their accomplishments are most impressive. In previous chapters we have referred to the techniques of Warden Watkins as an example of how a highly skilled person can manage the inmate culture by a shrewd application of both sociological theory and behavior modification techniques. However, the Warden's case also provides an illustration of the basic weakness in an excessive reliance upon casework as the primary treatment strategy.

First, there are not enough caseworkers to make the needed impact upon our correctional system. Warden Watkins is atypical in the amount of skill and energy that he was able to apply to the institution he commanded was extraordinary. But realistically it should be noted that the rest of his staff was primarily concerned with custody—that the Warden was probably the only skilled caseworker attempting to deal with some 700 inmates in that particular setting.

Second, as we noted, Warden Watkins eventually left the Draper Correctional Institution to take a better position. This illustrates another problem with a heavy reliance upon the casework approach in corrections. Those persons who are so highly skilled and motivated that they can successfully employ the complicated casework techniques also have the capacity to perform comparable functions that society rewards more liberally: they find that they need not spend their lives "serving time" in the dreary and frustrating settings of our penal institutions.

Reliance upon the development of correctional policy as opposed to depending upon caseworkers appears to us to be the only feasible way of dealing with crime on a scale large enough to have the impact that will soon be demanded by a body of taxpayers who are pouring billions of tax dollars into the criminal justice system. Policy measures such as the resurrection of the NAB program can be relatively easily implemented and designed to have a widespread impact without the limitations imposed by the lack of sufficient practitioners who have years of training and experience in casework methods.[10]

Notes to Chapter 6

1. Malcolm Braly, *On The Yard* (Boston: Little, Brown, 1967), p. 78.

2. See: Harold Padfield and Roy Williams, *Stay Where You Were: A Study of Unemployables in Industry* (Philadelphia: J. B. Lippincott, 1973).

3. New York State Special Commission on Attica, *Attica: The Official Report* (New York: Praeger, 1972), p. 53.

4. Padfield and Williams, pp. 143-173.

5. Susan Negrotto, "National Council on Crime and Delinquency Policy Statements and Model Acts," *Crime and Delinquency Literature* 4 (September 1972): 443.

6. Bernard B. Berk, "Organizational Goals and Inmate Organization," *American Journal of Sociology* 71 (March 1966): 522-534.

7. *Ibid.*

8. *Ibid.*

9. See: Roy Gerard, "Institutional Innovations in Juvenile Corrections," *Federal Probation* 34 (December 1970): 37-44.

10. For additional debate on the issue of shifting away from a heavy reliance upon casework, we recommend an article by two of our colleagues: Charles S. Prigmore and John C. Watkins, Jr., "Correctional Manpower: Are We 'The Society of Captives'?," *Federal Probation* 36 (December 1972): 12-19.

Bibliography

American Correctional Association. *Directory of Correctional Institutions and Agencies: 1971.* College Park, Md.: American Correctional Association, 1972.

Bennett, James V. *I Chose Prison.* New York: Alfred A. Knopf, 1970.

Berk, Bernard B. "Organizational Goals and Inmate Organization," *American Journal of Sociology* 71 (March 1966): 522-534.

Blake, James. *The Joint.* Garden City, N.Y: Doubleday, 1971.

Braly, Malcolm. *On the Yard.* Boston: Little, Brown, 1967.

Bryan, Helen. *Inside.* Boston: Houghton Mifflin, 1953.

Buffum, Peter C. *Homosexuality in Prisons.* Washington: U.S. Government Printing Office, 1972.

Burnham, Creighton Brown. *Born Innocent.* Englewood Cliffs, N.J: Prentice-Hall, 1958.

Burns, Henry, Jr. "A Miniature Totalitarian State: Maximum Security Prison," *The Canadian Journal of Corrections* 9 (July 1969): 153-164.

Cahn, William. "Report on the Nassau County Jail," *Crime and Delinquency* 19 (January 1973): 1-14.

Clemmer, Donald. *The Prison Community.* 2d ed., rev. New York: Holt, Rinehart and Winston, 1958.

Cloward, Richard A., and others. *Theoretical Studies in Social Organization of the Prison.* New York: Social Science Research Council, 1960.

Cressey, Donald R., ed. *The Prison: Studies in Institutional Organization and Change.* New York: Holt, Rinehart and Winston, 1966.

Elli, Frank. *The Riot.* New York: Coward, McCann & Geoghegan, 1966.

Fisher, Florrie. *The Lonely Trip Back.* Garden City, N.Y: Doubleday, 1971.

Gagon, John H., and Simon, William. "The Social Meaning of Prison Homosexuality," *Federal Probation* 32 (March 1968): 23-29.

Garfinkel, Harold. "Conditions of Successful Degradation Ceremonies," *American Journal of Sociology* 61 (March 1956): 420-424.

155

Gerard, Roy. "Institutional Innovations in Juvenile Corrections," *Federal Probation* 34 (December 1970): 37-44.

Giallombardo, Rose. *Society of Women: A Study of a Women's Prison.* New York: John Wiley and Sons, 1966.

——. "Social Roles in a Prison for Women," *Social Problems* 13 (Winter 1966): 268-288.

Gill, Howard B. "A New Prison Discipline: Implementing the Declaration of Principles of 1870," *Federal Probation* 34 (June 1970): 29-33.

Glasser, William. *Reality Therapy: A New Approach to Psychiatry.* New York: Harper and Row, 1965.

Griswold, H. Jack, and others. *An Eye for an Eye.* New York: Pocket Books, 1971.

Halleck, Seymour L., and Hersko, Marvin. "Homosexual Behavior in a Correctional Institution for Adolescent Girls," *American Journal of Orthopsychiatry* 32 (October 1962): 911-927.

Harris, Sara. *Hellhole.* New York: E. P. Dutton, 1967.

Hayner, Norman S. "Washington State Correctional Institutions as Communities," *Social Forces* 21 (March 1943): 316-322.

Haynes, F. E. "The Sociological Study of the Prison Community," *The Journal of Criminal Law and Criminology* 39 (November-December 1948): 432-440.

Heffernan, Esther. *Making It in Prison: The Square, the Cool, and the Life.* New York: Wiley-Interscience, 1972.

Heilbroner, Robert L. *The Economic Problem.* 2d ed. Englewood Cliffs, N.J: Prentice-Hall, 1970.

Illinois Department of Public Safety. *Menard: Illinois State Penitentiary.* Menard, Illinois (not dated).

Irwin, John. *The Felon.* Englewood Cliffs, N.J: Prentice-Hall, 1970.

——, and Cressey, Donald R. "Thieves, Convicts, and the Inmate Culture," *Social Problems* 10 (Fall 1962): 142-155.

Johnson, Elmer H. *Crime, Correction and Society.* Homewood, Ill: Dorsey Press, 1964.

——. "Sociology of Confinement: Assimilation and The Prison 'Rat'," *Journal of Criminal Law, Criminology and Police Science* 51 (January-February 1961): 528-533.

Johnson, Lester Douglas. *The Devil's Front Porch.* Lawrence, Kan: University Press of Kansas, 1970.

Kelley, Joanne. *When the Gates Shut.* London: Longmans, Green, 1967.

Kosofsky, Sidney, and Ellis, Albert. "Illegal Communication Among Institutionalized Female Delinquents," *The Journal of Social Psychology* 48 (August 1958): 155-160.

Lamson, David. *We Who Are About to Die.* New York: Charles Scribner's Sons, 1936.

LeClair, Edward E., Jr., and Schneider, Harold K. *Economic,* ed. *Anthropology: Readings in Theory and Analysis.* New York: Holt, Rinehart and Winston, 1968.

McManus, Virginia. *Not for Love.* New York: G.P. Putnam's Sons, 1960.

Minton, Robert J., Jr., ed. *Inside: Prison American Style.* New York: Random House, 1971.

Morris, Terence, and Morris, Pauline. *Pentonville: A Sociological Study of an English Prison.* London: Routledge and Kegan Paul, 1963.

Murton, Tom, and Hyams, Joe. *Accomplices to the Crime.* New York: Grove Press, 1970.

Nash, Manning. *Primitive and Peasant Economic Systems.* San Francisco: Chandler, 1966.

Neese, Robert. *Prison Exposures.* Philadelphia: Chilton, 1959.

Negrotto, Susan. "National Council on Crime and Delinquency Policy Statements and Model Acts," *Crime and Delinquency Literature* 4 (September 1972): 442-447.

New York State Special Commission on Attica. *Attica: The Official Report.* New York: Praeger, 1972.

Oswald, Russell G. *Attica: My Story.* Garden City, N.Y: Doubleday, 1972.

Padfield, Harold, and Williams, Roy. *Stay Where You Were: A Study of Unemployables in Industry.* Philadelphia: J.B. Lippincott, 1973.

Pell, Eve, ed. *Maximum Security: Letters from Prison.* New York: E.P. Dutton, 1972.

Piven, Herman, and Alcabes, Abraham. *Correctional Institutions.* Vol. II. Washington, D.C: U.S. Government Printing Office, 1969.

Roebuck, Julian B. *Criminal Typology.* Springfield, Ill: Charles C. Thomas, 1967.

Sands, Bill. *My Shadow Ran Fast.* Englewood Cliffs, N.J.: Prentice-Hall, 1964.

Sigler, Robert T. "A Study of Informal Peer Group Leaders," Unpublished Master's Thesis, Center for the Study of Crime, Delinquency and Corrections, Southern Illinois University, 1969.

Sykes, Gresham M. *The Society of Captives.* Princeton, N.J: Princeton University Press, 1971.

Taylor, A.J.W. "The Significance of 'Darls' or 'Special Relationships' for Borstal Girls," *The British Journal of Criminology* 5 (October 1965): 406-419.

Thomas, Piri. *Down These Mean Streets.* New York: Alfred A. Knopf, 1967.

Tittle, Charles R. "Inmate Organization: Sex Differentiation and the Influence of Criminal Subcultures," *American Sociological Review* 34 (August 1969): 492-505.

———, and Tittle, Drollene P. "Social Organization of Prisoners: An Empirical Test," *Social Forces* 43 (December 1964): 216-221.

U.S. Joint Commission on Correctional Manpower and Training. *A Time to Act.* Washington, D.C: Joint Commission on Correctional Manpower and Training, 1969.

The President's Commission on Law Enforcement and Administration of Justice, Task Force on Organized Crime. *Task Force Report: Organized Crime.* Washington, D.C: U.S. Government Printing Office, 1967.

Ward, David A., and Kassebaum, Gene G. *Women's Prison: Sex and Social Structure.* Chicago: Aldine, 1965.

Watkins, John Cleveland. "The Modification of the Subculture in a Correctional Institution." Presented before the 94th Congress of Correction, Kansas City, Missouri, September 1, 1964. (Mimeographed.)

Watkins, John Cummings, Jr., and Prigmore, Charles S. "Correctional Manpower: Are We 'The Society of Captives'?" *Federal Probation* 36 (December 1972): 12-19.

Wheeler, Stanton. "Socialization in Correctional Communities," *American Sociological Review* 26 (October 1961): 697-712.

Williams, Vergil Lewis. "Administration of Criminal Justice: A Bibliographical Selection," *Choice* 9 (July-August 1972): 611-618.

Williams, Vergil Lewis, and Fish, Mary. "Rehabilitation and Economic Self-Interest," *Crime and Delinquency* 16 (October 1970): 434-439.

———. "Optimum Prison Size: Cost Behavior vs. Rehabilitation Goals," *American Journal of Correction* 34 (March-April 1972): 14-19.

———. "The Token Economy in Prison: Rehabilitation or Motivation?" *Journal of Correctional Education* 24 (Fall 1972): 4-7.

Zimmerman, Erich W. *World Resources and Industries.* Rev. ed. New York: Harper & Row, 1951.

Index

About the Authors

Vergil L. Williams is Assistant Professor of Criminal Justice at The University of Alabama. His main teaching interests are in the area of law enforcement and penology. He received his Ph.D. degree in Business Administration from The University of Alabama. Professor Williams did graduate work in criminal justice at the Center for Crime, Delinquency, and Corrections at Southern Illinois University and worked as a Patrol Sergeant for the Amarillo, Texas Police Department. He and Professor Fish have coauthored a number of journal articles and conference papers in the field of criminal justice.

Mary Fish is Professor of Economics in the Graduate School of Business of the College of Commerce and Business Administration at The University of Alabama. Her teaching and research interests center on macroeconomic theory and policy and the application of economics to criminal justice. Dr. Fish holds a Bachelor's of Business Administration from the University of Minnesota, a Master's of Business Administration from Texas Technological College and a Ph.D. in Economics from the University of Oklahoma. Dr. Fish is a past recipient of an American Association of University Women's fellowship and has worked for the states of Iowa and California and the United States Army in Tokyo, Japan.